Teaching Tenets of Faith in Worship

Teaching Tenets of Faith in Worship

Catechetical Learning: Instilling the Basics of Faith in the Context of Worship

James Åkerson

FOREWORD BY
Paul E. Detterman

RESOURCE *Publications* • Eugene, Oregon

TEACHING TENETS OF FAITH IN WORSHIP
Catechetical Learning: Instilling the Basics of Faith in the Context of Worship

Copyright © 2019 James Åkerson. All rights reserved. Except for brief quotations in critical publications or reviews, no part of this book may be reproduced in any manner without prior written permission from the publisher. Write: Permissions, Wipf and Stock Publishers, 199 W. 8th Ave., Suite 3, Eugene, OR 97401.

Resource Publications
An Imprint of Wipf and Stock Publishers
199 W. 8th Ave., Suite 3
Eugene, OR 97401

www.wipfandstock.com

PAPERBACK ISBN: 978-1-5326-6297-3
HARDCOVER ISBN: 978-1-5326-6298-0
EBOOK ISBN: 978-1-5326-6299-7

Manufactured in the U.S.A.

Contents

Foreword by Paul E. Detterman | vii
Preface | xv

1. God the Father | 1
2. God the Son / Christ | 5
3. God the Holy Spirit | 9
4. God in Trinity | 13
5. God's Creation | 17
6. Sin & Death | 21
7. Mercy/Grace/Salvation | 25
8. God's Mission | 29
9. Faith/Baptism | 33
10. Scripture | 37
11. God's Church | 41
12. The Commands—1 | 45
13. The Commands—2 | 49
14. Our Lord's Prayer | 52
15. Confession | 55
16. Reform to Follow Christ | 58
17. Discerning the Way | 62
18. Communion and Washing Feet | 65
19. God's Gifted People | 69
20. Called Out of the World | 73

CONTENTS

21 In Thanks—1: Open Hands | 77
22 In Thanks—2: Stewardship | 81
23 Justice with Peace | 84
24 What We Await | 88
    Epilogue—Why We Teach Tenets of Faith | 92

Bibliography | 107
About the Author | 113

Foreword

> Sing praise to God who reigns above, the God of all creation,
> the God of power, the God of love, the God of our salvation.
> With healing balm my soul is filled,
> and every faithless murmur stilled:
> To God all praise and glory.[1]

In Psalm 139 we read, "You [God] made all the delicate, inner parts of my body and knit me together in my mother's womb. Thank you for making me so wonderfully complex! Your workmanship is marvelous—how well I know it." (Psalm 139:13-14 NLT)

This text is dedicated to conveying faith in a context of full-bodied worship. The Bible tells us that singing pleases God. One of the core documents in the Reformed Tradition, the Westminster Shorter Catechism, begins with the question: "What is the chief [purpose] of [humanity]?" The answer, "To glorify God and to enjoy him forever."[2] If you want to enjoy someone, you try to find out the things that bring *them* joy—the things that are important to them. Clearly beauty is vitally important to God; the beauty he creates in nature, the beauty he creates in the technical intricacies of all levels of the universe, the beauty he inspires in art, and movement, and music. God has created each of us to enjoy and to create beauty. That capability is sewn into every fiber of our being just as it is evident in every aspect of the visible world. Of all the

---

1. "Schütz, "Sei Lob," 59.
2. "The Westminster Shorter Catechism," 205.

FOREWORD

beauty and all the art forms in the world, the Bible most frequently commands God's people to sing!

> Come, let us sing to the Lord,
> Let us shout joyfully to the Rock of our salvation.
> (Psalm 95:1 NLT)

Consider a brief excerpt from a book by Keith and Kristyn Getty, the gifted couple who have written so many well-known contemporary hymns, among them "In Christ Alone."

> In C. S. Lewis' *The Magician's Nephew*, the great lion Aslan creates Narnia by singing it into existence. The character and timbre of the song are seen in the shapes and colors of all that springs up out of nothingness. Lewis delights to point out that the song could not be separated from the Singer. He eclipsed everything else. We are created to sing because it leads joyfully to the great Singer, Creator of the heavens and earth.[3]

In the same spirit, author and pastor Paul Tripp writes:

> God is the ultimate musician. His music transforms your life. The notes of redemption rearrange your heart and restore your life. His songs of grace, forgiveness, reconciliation, truth, hope, sovereignty, and love give you back your humanity and restore your identity.[4]

All of us can sing. Maybe not all of us sing perfectly or entirely on pitch, and some people are far more accomplished than others, but all of us can sing. That is how God knit us together. We are a singing people, and when we sing we join with the rest of God's creation, " . . . the music of the spheres."[5] There is no other activity that everyone (short of specific physical limitation) can do as naturally. Singing is written into our DNA.

---

3. Getty, *Sing!* 10.
4. Tripp, *A Quest for Something More*, 145.
5. Babcock, "This Is My Father's World," stanza 1.

FOREWORD

Not only that, but we are attuned to the words we sing. It has been suggested that 99 percent of people remember far more words set to music than they can recite Scripture from memory.[6]

Throughout much of the history of the Church, followers of Jesus have found great comfort, peace, assurance, strength, and joy in singing our faith together. No matter who leads worship, the "ultimate choir" at any church is the congregation—the people from various backgrounds and beliefs who, with a wide range of musical ability, blend voices together singing their shared praise to God.

While the planners and presenters of worship are the primary audience for this book, its focus is on that ultimate choir—what the congregation sings and says to God, and more importantly, why. Åkerson's desire is to guide worship planners in the selection of congregational text and song to teach the Christian faith.

Music for worship must be evaluated to see if it conveys the desired result. If what we sing in worship is vitally important, if music really does re-enforce memory, if the words we sing really do matter greatly, then it is important to look closely and critically at the text of any hymn or worship song and consider questions like these:

- "Who" is speaking?
- To whom?
- What or who is the topic?
- Why?
- What is the desired outcome or action?
- Is our focus being directed to the worship of God?

Take as an example the hymn stanza found at the beginning of this forward. It is a classic hymn text that is currently published in 161 hymnals.[7]

---

6. Getty, *Sing!* 2.
7. https://hymnary.org/text/sing_praise_to_god_who_reigns_above.

FOREWORD

> Sing praise to God who reigns above, the God of all creation,
> the God of power, the God of love, the God of our salvation.
> With healing balm my soul is filled
> and every faithless murmur stilled:
> To God all praise and glory.

- Who is speaking? The members of the congregation—the "ultimate choir."
- To whom? We are singing to each other, much in the spirit of Ephesians 5:19-20.
- What or who is the topic? An invitation to sing God's praise.
- Why? In one stanza we are reminded that God is omnipotent, God is love, God is the Lord of all creation and, amazingly, God has such focused compassion that he brings healing and comfort to an individual worshiper/singer—a mini-course in Christian theology in a few short lines!
- What is the desired outcome? It is to encourage each other to be extravagant and exuberant in our worship.
- Is the focus on God? Absolutely!

By contrast, look at the first verse of "Good, Good Father," currently one of the top five most popular worship songs as reported by Christian Copyright Licensing International (CCLI).[8]

- Who is speaking? It is an anonymous individual.
- To whom? God.
- What or who is the topic? God's disposition.
- Why? A monologue with God.
- What is the intended outcome? Feeling good about the individual's relationship with God.
- Is our focus being directed to the worship of God? Partially, though the more pronounced focus is on the fact that the individual is loved by God—that is their reality.

---

8. Brown and Barrett, "Good, Good Father," https://songselect.ccli.com/Songs/7036612/good-good-father.

This comparison has nothing to do with musical style, the factor around which many current worship decisions are being made. It does illustrate that text matters. Both of these texts have their place in the worship life of *individual* followers of Jesus, but each text also has intended and, possibly, unintended consequences in the worship life of a *congregation*. Each text teaches something very different about our relationship to God. The Schütz hymn encourages a universally accessible attitude of self-less praise, nurturing people in selflessness irrespective of their current life circumstances or depth of faith. Everyone can take part in that text. By contrast, the Brown/Barrett song relies on the personal experience of an individual believer that may or may not be the experience of a significant number of worshipers at a given worship gathering. In the context of this book, the Schütz hymn teaches us about God. The Brown/Barrett song is significantly more therapeutic and ultimately self-affirming.

Theology vs. therapy. Orthodoxy vs. Deism.

Åkerson's focus is on the re-enforcement of orthodox Christianity, specifically as we come head-to-head with a culture that is far more comfortable with therapeutic self-affirmation. His work follows the intentional exegesis of his particular congregation and faith tradition. He would be the first to remind you that his particular choices reflect the ethos of that community of faith. What may be more universally gleaned from this material is three-fold: first, the opportunity that the corporate worship of God presents for the intentional catechesis of any worshiping congregation; second, the reality that the choices we make in selecting the elements of worship should not only speak to the congregation we *have*, but can also impact the faith of the congregation God *is creating*; and third, the crucial role of music (sung texts) in that ongoing theological and spiritual formation.

Establishing the liturgical catechesis of a congregation is much like establishing the nutritional health of any group of people. The worship planner/lead worshiper is, in essence, the local theological dietitian. No dietitian would ask, "What foods do you like to eat?" and follow a diet plan laden with "favorites" simply to appease the peoples' palates. Those in their charge would soon exhibit symptoms of excess in some areas and nutritional depletion in others, and their long-term health would be compromised. So it is that a worship planner exhibits extreme negligence when s/he simply falls back on the "songs they really like to sing" irrespective of the theme or focus of worship on any given day, or the theology those texts continuously teach and re-enforce. As asserted above, the portion of the Good News that is being communicated in worship at any worship gathering has a far better chance of being remembered if correlative words are sung in one or several different ways—especially if those words can be sung in a style of music that reflects the prevailing culture of the congregation.

Careful worship planning not only reflects a congregation's current spiritual formation, but supports the long-term trajectory of the congregation's theological and spiritual growth. A rule of thumb for the directors of church choirs has been 70/30: the music planned for a choir in any given year includes 70 percent music they sang in previous years and 30 percent music that is new to them. Over the course of a few years, they will have doubled their musical and theological resources. In much the same way, the music and texts that are chosen for the "ultimate choir" can include 70 percent or so of the hymns, psalms, and spiritual songs they already know and love, and roughly 30 percent that are new to them, whether those are classic hymns they have not yet learned, global songs that convey a common gospel truth in a different idiom, or newly written songs that proclaim God's truth in fresh new ways. By doing this, lead worshipers can shape the theology and influence the practical faith of the worshipers in ways that are both comfortable and fresh.

As Åkerson entered into this project, it was with the heart of a pastor deeply concerned about shaping the theology and influencing the practical faith of his Virginia Anabaptist congregation. As you consider the materials that follow, do so in light of the habits and the heart-songs, the history and the trajectory of the specific people God has called you to serve. What does their worship proclaim about the amazing truth that a cosmic God became a human being in order that his human children could know and experience his redeeming grace and astonishing love?

God bless you in this awesome calling!

The Reverend Dr. Paul Detterman

Senior Pastor, The First Presbyterian Church
of River Forest, Illinois

September 17, 2018

Preface

American Christians live in a culture with a host of media promoting a variety of religious and anti-religious thought through modern and post-modern thinking. As a result, many Christians' faith is muddled and leans to a syncretism of orthodox and unorthodox beliefs. A sociological study of over 3000 young people by Smith and collaborators through the years indicates that American Christian orthodoxy has degraded to the point that a majority of youth and their parents think the essence of faith is to believe in God, be happy, and be nice.[1] Smith declares that "Christianity is actively being colonized and displaced by a quite different religious faith . . . We have come with some confidence to believe that a significant part of 'Christianity' in the United States is actually only tenuously connected to the actual historic Christian tradition, but has rather substantially morphed into Christianity's misbegotten step-cousin, Christian Moralistic Therapeutic Deism."[2] The general situation is not new. As early as the 15th century, Erasmus wrote about the need for Christian religious training. About him one researcher said, "Erasmus believed the greatest concern of his time was that many individuals who considered themselves to be Christians were ignorant of true faith, and actually were 'rank heathens.'"[3]

1. Smith and Denton, *Soul Searching*, 162-163, 262.
2. Smith, "On 'Moralistic Therapeutic Deism,'" https://www.ptsem.edu/uploadedFiles/School_of_Christian_Vocation_and_Mission/Institute_for_Youth_Ministry/Princeton_Lectures/Smith-Moralistic.pdf.
3. Graffagnino, "The Shaping of the Two Earliest Anabaptist Catechisms," 45.

PREFACE

Through the centuries, pastors and teachers have attempted to teach their followers the elements of faith in pre-baptismal and confirmation (catechism) classes. That is still typically the practice today, but such teaching is often the last systematic instruction that believers receive in their faith life. For most of us, what follows baptism or confirmation is a hodge-podge of unrelated sermons and Bible studies. As for special Bible studies to periodically instruct the faithful on elements of faith, there is growing realization among church catechists that attendance at Sunday schools, vacation Bible schools, and catechism classes is falling.[4] Much is written about the frenetic lives of Americans. Perhaps those busy lives translate into unwillingness to commit to "one more set of meetings." It is well then that preachers and worship leaders regularly cover specific elements of faith in their words for worship and sermons.

This catechetical lectionary with worship planning aids was created to help congregations and individuals better grasp the historical orthodox tenets of their faith. Just as it is not sufficient for any of us to be taught something once, expecting we will retain it forever, the tool should be used on a periodical basis to remind and clarify our grasp of the Christian faith. It is up to preachers and worship leaders to re-enforce the basic tenets of faith in regular worship. As believers, we would do well to consider such faith training like continuing education as in our professions and workplaces.

Many preachers have attempted theological preaching series. What is presented here, however, is not only a sermon series but a robust worship setting that incorporates thematic theological ideas, from the opening welcome to the ending benediction. Among educators multi-intelligence theory advocates instruction that reaches the intellect, emotions, and senses such as hearing, touch, and smell, among others.[5] Instruction in the context of worship has

---

4. Watson, "Sunday School is Dying," 5; Buegler, "Why Is No One Talking About This?" https://elcaymnet.wordpress.com/2013/12/02/why-is-no-one-talking-about-this/.

5. Kohler, "Preaching the Gospel to All," all.

PREFACE

great potential for utilizing these facets by reaching the intellect, heart, emotions, and soul of the worshiper. There is also growing appreciation for the need to teach with several methods to adequately motivate students' personality and learning types.[6]

As a caution against heavy-handed teaching amid worship, the literature indicates that if preaching is conducted with pedantic instruction, it negatively affects participants' worship experience.[7] It appears that it is not the content itself but the nature of teaching that is most objectionable to worshippers. Maintaining the mystery and joy of worship is essential while providing appropriate content. Serious orthodoxy must be interspersed with a light touch throughout the worship service so that worshipers are not distracted from the Holy Spirit[8] while still conveying the thematic theological understanding for the day.

This catechetical lectionary covers twenty-four Sundays of "Ordinary Time" in the Church calendar to present basic aspects of Christian faith. As envisioned, it is set in the spring, summer, and fall of a year, beginning with the first Sunday after Pentecost. The full period of Ordinary Time is a little longer than the proposed lectionary. Other Sundays, including three winter Sundays of Ordinary Time, are intentionally left unclaimed to provide flexibility in the worship schedule to accommodate local church events and to include additional aspects of denominational teaching. Practitioners from outside the Anabaptist tradition might substitute appropriate denominational creedal statements for those provided here in the "Profession" sections of each chapter.

James Åkerson

---

6. Dirkx, "Transformative Learning Theory in the Practice of Adult Education," https://www.iup.edu/WorkArea/DownloadAsset.aspx?id=18335.

7. DeVillers, *Lectionary-based Catechesis for Children*, 3; Dooley, "The Lectionary as a Sourcebook of Catechesis," 42.

8. Dooley, "Remembering The Future," 3.

1

God the Father

Introduction:

Moses met God alone in the Midian desert. After 40 years of exile from Egypt, God approached the fugitive saying, "I am the God of your father, the God of Abraham, the God of Isaac, and the God of Jacob" (Exod 3:6). Even with that introduction Moses realized that he did not know the name of the God of his people. When he posed his question, God answered him, "I Am Who I Am," and "I Am" (Exod 3:14). Our understanding of God is shrouded in unknowing as well. We speak of God as God, which is both honorific and ignorant. There is remedy. God may be known by God's attributes—it is perhaps the best way for puny human minds to know and understand the true and One God Almighty.

Theme:

We know God by God's attributes.

Scripture:

Exodus 3:13–15; 20:1–6; 34:5–7 / Deuteronomy 6:4

Psalm 25:4–10; 68:5

1 John 4:7–12, 16

Matthew 5:48

TEACHING TENETS OF FAITH IN WORSHIP

Preaching Points:

The attributes of God

Helpful Sources:

Confession of Faith (1995),[1] Article 1

Global Anabaptists,[2] #1

The Attributes of God, Volume I[3]

Claiming Faith,[4] session 2

Heidelberg Catechism,[5] #6, 11–12, 26

What We Believe Together,[6] 19–36

New City,[7] 12–13

Presbyterian Q/A,[8] 27

Luther's Small Catechism,[9] Part II–Creed, First Article of Creation

Suggested Hymns/Worship Songs:

Holy, holy, holy (v. 1, 2, 6)

All people that on earth do dwell

Great is the Lord

---

1. General Board of the General Conference Mennonite Church, *Confession of Faith in a Mennonite Perspective*, article 1.
2. "Shared Convictions of Global Anabaptists," #1.
3. Tozer, *The Attributes of God*, Volume I.
4. Mennonite Church USA, *Claim(ing) Faith*, session 2.
5. Christian Reformed Church, "The Heidelberg Catechism," #6, 11–12, 26.
6. Neufeld, *What We Believe Together*, 19–36.
7. Keller and Shammas, *New City Catechism*, 12–13.
8. McKim, *Presbyterian Questions, Presbyterian Answers*, 27.
9. Stump, *An Explanation of Luther's Small Catechism*, Part-II.

GOD THE FATHER

God of grace and God of glory

Immortal, invisible, God only wise

All creatures of our God and King

Bluegrass gospel motif (B/G): Farther Along

B/G: He's Right On Time

Call to Worship:

L: Come. Worship the King!

P: It is right to praise the Lord Our God.

L: Come. Find your way to the Assembly of Believers.

P: It is right to worship God the Father with singing and praise!

Confession and Absolution:

L: Father, you created us for your fellowship.

P: Please forgive us for neglecting our time with you.

L: Father, please forgive our hiding from you.

P: Forgive us and bring us into fellowship so that we may learn and walk in your ways.

[Moment for silent confession]

L: Draw us to yourself and fill us with desire to please you.

All: Thank you Lord God, our Father, for your mercy. Please walk with us so that we may know you and become more like you.

L: God promised "*If we confess our sins, he is faithful and just and will forgive us our sins and purify us from all unrighteousness.*" People of God, you can live in newness of life.

Offering Prayer:

Lord Our God, you are wholly good, and full of justice and mercy. Your graciousness to all things is seen in nature, and the seasons, and in scripture. Please fill us with your great love and help us to grow the desire to be like you, full of mercy and grace toward others, both here and far away. Amen.

Benediction:

As Isaiah proclaimed, may you go out in joy, and be led back in peace; may the mountains and the hills before you burst into song; and may all the trees of the field clap their hands in praise of our Lord, God and Father.[10]

---

10. Isa 55:12.

2
God the Son / Christ

Introduction:

People know of Jesus Christ, perhaps thinking it denotes his given name and surname, as with people today. Learning of his given name and title helps us better understand the nature, character, and work of Jesus.

Themes:

Christ is God.

Christ fulfills several eternal roles such as Messiah/Christ, Savior, Lord, High Priest, Sacrificial Lamb, and Judge.

Scripture:

Isaiah 40:1–11 / Isaiah 11

Psalm 2

Hebrews 1–3; 4:14–5:10; 7–10 / Romans 3:21–26 / Colossians 1:15–17

John 1; 5:19–29; 15:1–17 / Matthew 16:1–20; 23:37

Preaching Points:

Messiah / Christ

Lamb of God

Lord

Son of Man (Ezekiel, Daniel, gospels) / Son of God (what others said of him in gospels and epistles, except in Jesus' words of John's gospel)

Helpful Sources:

Confession of Faith (1995), Article 2

Global Anabaptists, #2

The Attributes of God, Volume 1

God's Story,[1] ch. 4

Claiming Faith, session 2

Heidelberg Catechism, #29–52

What We Believe Together, 37–58

New City, 48–57, 102–107

Presbyterian Q/A, 29–36

Luther's Small Catechism, Part II–Creed, Second Article of Redemption

Suggested Hymns/Songs:

Joy to the world

All hail the power of Jesus' name

Crown him with many crowns

Fairest Lord Jesus

Jesus, thy blood and righteousness

Worthy is the Lamb

---

1. Hershberger, *God's Story, Our Story*, ch. 4.

What a friend we have in Jesus

B/G: Good News

B/G: Purple Robe

Call to Worship:

L: Hail the power of Jesus' name!

P: We praise you, Lord Jesus Christ.

L: Praise our Lord and King.

P: You call us to worship, Lord Jesus. We praise you.

L: Our Lord promised to join those that gather in his name.

All: Thank you Lord Jesus Christ. You are the One that brings us life and hope and joy. We call upon your powerful name, Lord Jesus Christ.

Confession and Absolution:

L: Lord Jesus Christ, you call us to live lives of great hope and love.

P: Please forgive us for closing our eyes to your love.

L: Lord Jesus Christ, you call us to speak of what we know of you with others.

P: Please forgive us for stopping up our hearts and mouths.

L: Dear Lord Jesus Christ, prepare our hearts to meet you.

[Moment for silent confession]

L: Lord Jesus Christ, you call us to live lives of service to others and all creation.

P: Please help move us from thinking only of ourselves.

All: You are the One that makes our hope and joy in life possible. Thank you for your great love, Lord Jesus Christ.

L: As we confess our sins, God is merciful and just to forgive us all our unrighteousness. Live in newness of life.

Offering Prayer:

Lord Jesus Christ, it is through you that we have life and hope and joy. Help us to understand that all life depends on your mercy and grace. Grow our hearts so that we are as open-handed with possessions as you were in giving them to us. We thank you now with our gifts. Amen.

Benediction:

As scripture says: Now to him who is able to keep you from falling, and to make you stand without blemish in the presence of his glory with rejoicing, to the only God our Savior through Jesus Christ our Lord, be glory, majesty, power, and authority, before all time and now and forever. Amen.[2]

---

2. Jude 24–25.

3

God the Holy Spirit

Introduction:

Interest in the Holy Spirit seems to run hot or cold among one denomination and another. What C. S. Lewis said about Aslan (his Christ-figure) not being a tame lion might certainly be said about God's Holy Spirit. The Spirit is not to be contained and controlled. Some people are frightened by the prospect of not knowing if a movement of the spirit is of the Holy Spirit; discernment is required. Some people are pleased to see God's actions and presence among us today. In their minds they can enjoy that some stories of God are not relegated to yesteryear and long ago.

Themes:

God's Holy Spirit is purveyor of grace.

God's Holy Spirit is our counselor and guide.

Scripture:

Isaiah 63:7–14

Psalm 139

Acts 1:16; 2:4, 17–18; 5:32 / Romans 7:5–6; 8:1–5, 9, 26 / 1 Corinthians 12:1–14 / James 4:4–6 / 2 Peter 1:19–21

Matthew 28:19 / Mark 1:8; 13:11 / John 14:26; 16:13

TEACHING TENETS OF FAITH IN WORSHIP

Preaching Points:

Omnipresence, mercy, grace, holiness

Nicene Creed

The Holy Spirit is our counselor, interpreter, and inspiration.

Helpful Sources:

Confession of Faith (1995), Article 3

Global Anabaptists, #3 & #5

The Attributes of God, Volume 1

God's Story, ch. 6

Claiming Faith, session 2

Heidelberg Catechism #53, 25, 65, 67, 69, 86

What We Believe Together, 59–72

New City, 80–82

Presbyterian Q/A, 45–47, 50–52

Luther's Small Catechism, Part II–Creed, Third Article of Sanctification

Suggested Hymns/Songs:

Breathe on me breath of God

Spirit of the living God

Spirit of God, descend upon my heart

Set my soul afire

Revive us again

Sweet, sweet Spirit

B/G: Just A Closer Walk

B/G: I Saw the Light

B/G: The Touch of God's Hand

Call to Worship:

L: Our Lord promised to be with us as we gather.

P: We come to worship the Lord our God. We thank you for the presence of your Holy Spirit to guide us.

All: Praise the Father, Son, and Holy Spirit.

Confession and Absolution:

L: Dear Lord, we have sinned.

P: We follow our own way and do not look for your Holy Spirit and the Way of Peace. Please forgive us.

L: We have not looked for signs of your Holy Spirit in our lives.

P: Please open our eyes. We find enemies every day and do not look for your image in everyone we meet. Help us to find hope.

[Moment of silent confession]

L: We look to you, Lord.

All: You are the One who can cure us from sin. You are the One who leads us to peace. Help us to follow your Spirit. Thank you for your presence. Amen.

L: God promised "*If we confess our sins, he is faithful and just and will forgive us our sins and purify us from all unrighteousness.*"[1] People of God, you can live in newness of life.

Offering Prayer:

We thank you, Lord, for your open-handed giving of everything we have. We thank you for the presence of your Holy

---

1. 1 John 1:9

Spirit among us. Help us be as open-handed in our thanks as you are with us every day. Thank you, Father, Son, and Holy Spirit. Amen.

Benediction:

May God's Holy Spirit fill you with hope, today and all through your week. May you find God's Spirit as you work in Christ's way of peace. The Lord bless you and keep you; the Lord make his face to shine upon you, and be gracious to you; the Lord lift up his countenance upon you, and give you peace. Amen.

4
God in Trinity

Introduction:

How can it be that God is both One and Three Persons? The answer is not an easy one. We Christian believers hold with the Jewish faith that there is One God, not a panoply of gods and demigods. Therefore God is God everywhere in the world. We Christian believers also hold that God the Father, Son, and Holy Spirit are of One spirit and purpose. They participate in and make up the one godhead of God Almighty, maker of all things.

Theme:

We worship One Holy God who is Father, Son, and Holy Spirit eternally.

Scripture:

Genesis 1–2; 3:20–24

Psalm 8

Romans 8:26 / Acts 10 / Ephesians 3:14–19 / 1 John 4:7–21 / 2 Corinthians 13:13

John 1:1–5, 14, 16, 18; 14:9; 16:12–15; 20:19–23 / Matthew 28:19

Preaching Points:

Though we confess that God is One in Three Persons, it is a mystery.

God's attributes are fully displayed in the Trinity of God.

We know God by what God shows us in Scripture and the inklings within us provided by God's Holy Spirit.

Helpful Sources:

Confession of Faith (1995), Article 1

Global Anabaptists, #1

The Attributes of God, Volume 1

Apostles' Creed

Nicene Creed

Heidelberg Catechism, #25–26

New City, 14–15

Presbyterian Q/A, 23–24

Luther's Small Catechism, Part II–Creed

Suggested Hymns/Songs:

Holy, holy

Holy, holy, holy

Come, thou Almighty King

Father, I adore you

Glorify thy name

B/G: [Do You Know the] Father, Son, and Holy Ghost

Call to Worship:

L: We worship you, Lord God Almighty.

P: We praise you Father; you are Creator and Sustainer of all things.

L: We worship you, Lord Jesus Christ.

P: We praise you Lord Jesus Christ, Creator, Shepherd, and Savior.

L: We worship you, Eternal One in Three; Thy Holy Spirit urges us onward.

P: We worship you, Father, Son, and Holy Spirit. You call the ungodly to be holy. You call humankind into fellowship. You guide and comfort believers each day of their lives.

All: We worship you Eternal One, Father, Son, and Holy Spirit.

Confession and Absolution:

L: Dear Lord God, we do not understand your ways.

P: You are too great for us to fully know.

L: Our selfishness leads us into sin.

P: Please forgive us.

L: We confess that we have sinned against you and against your creation.

[Moment for silent confession]

L: Thank-you, Lord God, for your gift of life.

P: Thank you, Lord Jesus, for saving us from our sin and for sending your Spirit to convict, comfort, and guide us.

All: Without your help, Eternal One in Three, we could not walk in your Way. Help us follow you faithfully.

L: 1 John 1:9 says, "If we confess our sins, he is faithful and just and will forgive us our sins and purify us from all unrighteousness." People of God, you can live secure in God's promise.

Offering Prayer:

Dear Lord God, you have created all things, and your Word makes them good. You created all creatures, waters, earth, and sky, all space, stars, and planets, and all the ingredients that make them possible. By your gracious hand you sustain us. Help us to be thankful and as open-handed with your gifts, and loving toward others, as you are with us. Amen.

Benediction:

Go in the power of God knowing you are loved. Go in the name of the Father, Son, and Holy Spirit with the mission to obey the Lord your God all the days of your lives.

5

God's Creation

Introduction:

God created all things. The how and timing of Creation is yet to be revealed since God says, "... do not forget this one thing, dear friends: With the Lord a day is like a thousand years, and a thousand years are like a day" (2 Peter 3:8). By the Genesis Creation accounts we know that God spoke and the things of Creation came to exist. We also know that God created all things good. The order of Creation, with its lack of chaos, indicates to us that all things will be made right in the eschatological end.

Theme:

God made all things good and declared them so.

Scripture:

Genesis 1–2 / Deuteronomy 4:32

Psalm 104; 136; 148

Colossians 1:15–17 / 1 Timothy 4:4

John 1:1–4, 9–11

Preaching Points:

God made all things.

God spoke and all was made.

God made and declared all things good.

Helpful Sources:

Confession of Faith (1995), Article 5

Global Anabaptists, #7

God's Story, ch. 1

Claiming Faith, sessions 2 & 3

Heidelberg Catechism, #26–28

New City, 16–17, 18-19, 60–61

Presbyterian Q/A, 25–26

Luther's Small Catechism, Part II–Creed, First Article of Creation

Suggested Practices:

Give an assignment to ponder five aspects of God's Creation through the week: darkness & light, physical/structural, biological/living, time, and spiritual.

Suggested Hymns/Songs:

Great is the Lord

All creatures of our God and King

All things bright and beautiful

All creatures of our God and King

Morning has broken

God's Creation

He's got the whole world in his hands

B/G: I Am a Pilgrim

B/G: The Touch of God's Hand

Call to Worship:

L: This is the day the Lord has made.

P: Let us rejoice and be glad in it.

L: God has made us.

P: God has made all things and all the elements to make all things.

All: Great is the Lord God Almighty, and Jesus Christ the Son, and God's Holy Spirit. God created us and we are the Lord's.

Confession and Absolution:

L: It is time to confess our sins.

P: Dear Lord God Almighty, we forget that you made us and we are yours. We are not our own. Please forgive us.

L: We have indeed acted as if we are gods, not bowing to your authority.

P: Please forgive us.

L: There are times that we forget that you gave us a job to cherish and care for your creation.

P: Please forgive us.

[Moment for silent confession]

L: The Lord God Almighty is merciful and just. God will forgive us our sin as we confess them. Walk now in newness of life, resolving to walk in holiness and obedience toward our God.

All: Thanks be to God.

Offering Prayer:

Dear Lord, your bounty and goodness are overwhelming and wonderful. Help us to be as open and willing to share your bounty as you are in giving them to us. We thank you for life and health, daily food, shelter, and our possessions. They are all from you. We praise your name, Father, Son, and Holy Spirit. Amen.

Benediction:

May the Lord reveal the gifts you have received from his hand. May you resolve to work as faithful stewards of all creation for our Lord Jesus Christ. Go in peace. Serve the Lord. Amen.

6

Sin & Death

Introduction:

All things were made right and good by the Lord God Almighty in Creation. From a simple narrative in Genesis, we learn from where temptation comes, that temptation acted out is sin, that sin draws us away from God, and that sin grown in fullness surely leads to death.

Themes:

Sin brings death and separation from God.

Sin does not destroy God's Creation, but it mars its unity, beauty, and grace.

Scripture:

Genesis 3; 6:11–12 / Exodus 20:1–21 / Isaiah 1:11–17

Psalm 14:1–3

Romans 1:18–32; 6:23 / Ephesians 2:1–3

Matthew 1:18–21; 6:9–15

Preaching Points:

Sin mars God's good Creation.

TEACHING TENETS OF FAITH IN WORSHIP

Without Christ, we are lost in corruption and sin.

Helpful Sources:

Confession of Faith (1995), Article 7

Global Anabaptists, #3

God's Story, ch. 4

Claiming Faith, session 4

Heidelberg Catechism, #3–10, 87

New City, 40–41, 44–45

Presbyterian Q/A, 26, 39–40, 42–43, 72

Suggested Practices:

Give an assignment for the week to ponder how sin is related to death: within our psyches/souls and bodies.

Suggested Hymns/Songs:

O come, O come, Emmanuel

Come, thou long-expected Jesus

I wonder as I wander

There is a balm in Gilead

Cleanse me

Come, thou fount of every blessing

B/G: I Saw the Light

B/G: Did Trouble Me

B/G: Stumbling Blocks

B/G: Never Give the Devil a Ride

Call to Worship:

L: People of God, we are called to worship the King, Who is Creator of all things good.

P: Let us draw near to God that we may know God.

L: Let us gather to worship the Lord.

P: Let us draw near to worship the Lord of lords, King of kings, and Creator of all.

Confession and Absolution:

L: People of God, we are called to worship the King and Creator of all, but sin creeps into our lives. Sin blurs our vision and desire to seek the things of the Kingdom.

P: O Lord, our God, we confess that we fall into sin. Help us to acknowledge our sin to you.

[Moment for silent confession]

L: People of God, sin leads only to death, but as we confess our sin, God the Father through Jesus Christ, in the power of the Holy Spirit, forgives us all our sin and unrighteousness. God draws us into fellowship.

All: Lord, help us willingly draw close to you that we may know your righteousness and desire to be made holy. We ask it in Jesus' powerful name. Amen.

Offering Prayer:

Dear Lord Jesus, sin and death are all around us. Help us to be faithful members of your army of followers. Help us be faithful examples of love and light and hope. We offer these gifts now as thank-offerings for all that you have given us. Amen.

Benediction:

Go now, people of God, knowing that God created all things good. Go, knowing that we are called to be faithful believers. Go, knowing that we are called to live and act entirely differently from the world. We are to live in love, joy, peace, patience, kindness, goodness, faithfulness, gentleness, and self-control. Go, in God's power. Amen.

7

Mercy/Grace/Salvation

Introduction:

It is indeed a great mercy that God provides a way for our restoration into fellowship with God. Through Jesus Messiah/Christ we can be healed of our sin sickness. God's grace allows our salvation from sin.

Theme:

In mercy and grace, God offers redemption from sin through Jesus Christ.

Scripture:

Exodus 34:1–7 / Isaiah 40 / Micah 6:8

Psalm 28; 136

Romans 3:21–26; 7:21–8:4 / 1 Timothy 1:12–16 / Hebrews 4:15–16

John 3:16–21

Preaching Points:

God loves the whole world.

God provided a way out of our sin predicament.

TEACHING TENETS OF FAITH IN WORSHIP

Everyone can come to God through his Holy Spirit; no one is prohibited.

We cannot earn salvation; Jesus Christ is the Way, the Truth, and the Life.

Mercy is not getting what we deserve. Grace is getting what we do not deserve.

Helpful Sources:

Confession of Faith (1995), Articles 7, 8

Global Anabaptists, #3

God's Story, ch. 5

Claiming Faith, session 4

Making Disciples,[1] sessions 5 & 6

Heidelberg Catechism, #11–20, 62

New City, 56–59, 78–79

Presbyterian Q/A, 50–52, 55

Suggested Practices:

Give an assignment for the week to ponder how salvation might free us to serve Jesus Christ.

Suggested Hymns/Songs:

Amazing grace

Behold, what manner of love

Great is thy faithfulness

Surely goodness and mercy

There's a wideness in God's mercy

1. Yamasaki, *Making Disciples*, sessions 5 and 6.

Thy loving kindness

B/G: Just A Closer Walk

B/G: I Saw the Light

B/G: He Took Your Place

B/G: Softly and Tenderly

Call to Worship:

L: There is an amazing wideness in God's mercy. Come, people of God. Come and worship the King.

P: Thanks be to God, the One that calls our name, and bids us into fellowship.

L: We gather together to sing of God's mercy.

All: We gather together to worship and adore the One that loves us. God is full of mercy and love, and will lead us into righteousness.

Confession and Absolution:

L: God invites us to confess our sin and call upon the name of Jesus Christ for salvation. We need not die in our sin.

P: Dear Lord, we confess that we have sinned by what we have done, by what we have left undone, and by our inner thoughts. There is no true, long-lasting good in us without you. Please forgive us our sin.

[Moment for silent confession]

L: We can rejoice. Those who call upon the Lord Jesus Christ and confess their sins will not die but find mercy and grace.

P: Thank you Father, Son, and Holy Spirit. You provide the way to righteousness. You alone are the One that calls us a holy people.

All: We pray for your gracious help to be and become your holy people.

Offering Prayer:

Dear Lord, it is mercy and grace that you desire from your holy people. Help us to be full of your mercy and love—showing the world your generous spirit. We ask that you bless these gifts to your work. In Jesus' name we pray. Amen.

Benediction:

Our great God of mercy and grace has shown us what is good, O people. And what does the Lord require of you? To act justly and to love mercy, and to walk humbly with your God.[2]

---

2. Micah 6:8.

8
God's Mission

Introduction:

Salvation from our sure, former pathway to death should grow in us such thankful hearts that we energetically participate in God's continuing mission to reach others (all peoples), and restore all things into God's glad, good status. We are not saved to grow fat in God's goodness. We are saved to work for "Thy Kingdom come, Thy Will be done on earth as it is in heaven."

Theme:

God's mission is to redeem all things. It is Good News for all peoples.

Scripture:

Exodus 6:2–6/ Isaiah 44:12–23

Psalm 96:1–3

Acts 1:6–9, 13:44–48 / Romans 10:9–15 / Galatians 5:22–23

Matthew 28:19–20; John 15:1–17; 20:19–23

TEACHING TENETS OF FAITH IN WORSHIP

Preaching Points:

> God sent Jesus Christ to redeem and reconcile the world to himself.
>
> As believers we are no longer slaves but sons and daughters, heirs of the King.
>
> We are called to proclaim the Good News of Jesus Christ in order to reconcile the world to God.

Helpful Sources:

> Confession of Faith (1995), Article 10
>
> Global Anabaptists, #7
>
> God's Story, ch. 8
>
> Claiming Faith, session 8
>
> Making Disciples, session 9
>
> Presbyterian Q/A, 68–70

Suggested Practices:

> Give an assignment for the week to ponder how we might be specifically called into God's mission as individuals, as families, and as a congregation.

Suggested Hymns/Songs:

> A charge to keep I have
>
> All creatures of our God and King
>
> Go tell it on the mountain
>
> Christ is made the sure foundation
>
> Doxology
>
> We've a story to tell to the nations

B/G: Working On A Building

B/G: Will There Be Any Stars in My Crown

Call to Worship:

L: Come, people of God; there's work to be done.

P: Come, let us worship the Lord as we prepare to serve our Lord.

Confession and Absolution:

L: People of God, sin mars our armor.

P: The Lord knows us. God knows our sin; and yet there is hope. God calls us a holy people, set aside for his service. Let us confess our sin that we may be made whole and complete to do God's work.

[Moment for silent confession]

L: People of God, our Lord God is merciful and just to forgive us all our unrighteousness as we confess our sin. Walk forward in newness of life to serve the Lord.

All: Praise be to God, the Almighty and Gracious. Help us now, Lord, to serve you well in Jesus' powerful name. Amen.

Offering Prayer:

In the entire world there is no god but you Lord, God Almighty. We thank you for your unending love. We revel in your wonderful mercy and grace. Help us, Lord Jesus, to resemble your personality of love, mercy, and grace. Thank you for all good gifts. Please accept these offerings as our thanks to you. We praise you, Lord Jesus Christ. Amen.

Benediction:

> L: Go now, people of God; may you return to your work in good cheer. Be the called and set-aside people of God—reconciling the world to God.
>
> P: We go—fitted for work in the Kingdom.
>
> L: There's work to be done!
>
> P: We go—in service to our Lord Jesus Christ.

9
Faith/Baptism

Introduction:

> God loves his Creation with no exceptions. Though we are not worthy of such love, God comes to us through the Holy Spirit to nudge us forward to recognize the pathway into fellowship with God's Self and other believers by faith in Jesus Christ. We are not called into solitude but into a fellowship. Even our response is by God's grace. We can give thanks and sing "Halleluiah" to the King of Kings.

Theme:

> The Holy Spirit leads us into faith, and we respond by dedicating our lives to Christ.

Scripture:

> Numbers 5:5–10
>
> Psalm 51:1–12
>
> Romans 3:21–26 / Hebrews 11 / James 1–2
>
> Matthew 23:23; 25:31–46; 28:18–20 / Mark 1:1–5 / Luke 3:3:9–11 / John 3:11; 14:21–24

TEACHING TENETS OF FAITH IN WORSHIP

Preaching Points:

Faith is the decision to follow Christ in a long, sustained manner.

Our faith is given and nurtured by the Holy Spirit.

Baptism is an outward sign of beginning to walk with Jesus Christ, as with marriage.

Faith carries us forward into actions for the Kingdom of God.

Helpful Sources:

Confession of Faith (1995), Articles 8, 11

Global Anabaptists, #3

God's Story, ch. 4 & 5

Claiming Faith, session 6

Making Disciples, session 1

Heidelberg Catechism, #20–24, 65, 67–73, 87

New City, 46–47, 56–59, 62–73, 93–95, 109–110

Presbyterian Q/A, 56–57, 79–80

Luther's Small Catechism, Part IV–The Sacrament of Holy Baptism

Suggested Practices:

Baptism during the worship service, if possible.

Give an assignment for the week to ponder what we must die to in order to be faithful to our baptism in Jesus Christ.

Suggested Hymns/Songs:

Just as I am

FAITH/BAPTISM

Take my life and let it be

Because he lives

I know whom I have believed

My faith looks up to thee

Take the name of Jesus with you

B/G: Softly and Tenderly

B/G: Good News

B/G: There's a Light at the River

Call to Worship:

L: All the people of the world are called to worship the Lord our God.

P: We come. We look to the heavens to find our Redeemer.

L: Jesus Christ has promised to gather with us as we worship.

P: Bless the Lord Jesus Christ. Bless Father, Son, and Holy Spirit. We come to worship the Lord.

Confession and Absolution:

L: The Apostle John said forcefully, "If we claim to be without sin, we deceive ourselves and the truth is not in us . . . If we claim we have not sinned, we make him out to be a liar and his word is not in us."[1] We are given the choice to confess our sins or to die in them.

P: Help us, Lord Jesus, to understand ourselves, and to know that we have sinned against you and against our neighbors.

L: Let us consider our lives and confess the sins that we know of to God.

---

1. 1 John 1:8, 10.

[Moment for silent confession]

L: In addition to the sins we know of, Scripture tells us that there is sin in us unknown even to ourselves.

All: Lord Jesus, please forgive us for all sin, those we did on purpose, those we did not intend, and those things we left undone.

L: The Apostle John said, "If we confess our sins, he is faithful and just and will forgive us our sins and purify us from all unrighteousness."[2]

All: Thanks be to God.

Offering Prayer:

Dear Father, everything we are, and everything we have, came from you. Thank you for your gift of life and health and food and shelter. Help us to be as generous with your gifts as you were in giving them to us. We praise you, giver of all good gifts. Amen.

Benediction:

May you, the people of God, go out into the world remembering that you are "in the world but not of it." God made all things good. Your job is to help lost ones find the way back into the loving arms of our Lord Jesus Christ. Go; knowing that God loves you and will be beside you as you work for the Kingdom.

---

2. 1 John 1:9.

10
Scripture

Introduction:

God's Word encompasses scripture and the true nudgings of God's Holy Spirit. We need the Holy Spirit to understand God's intent for our lives each day. A great joy in ongoing reading of the Bible is that the Holy Spirit leads us to recognize and comprehend different themes and messages for our lives, even within passages we might have read several times before. Indeed, it is God's living Word for our lives.

Theme:

Scripture is God's Word for life.

Scripture:

Daniel 9:2

Psalm 19

2 Timothy 3:16–17 / Acts 17:2 / Romans 15:4 / 1 Timothy 4:13 / 2 Peter 1:19–21

Matthew 21:42

Teaching Tenets of Faith in Worship

Preaching Points:

"All Scripture is God-breathed and is useful for teaching, rebuking, correcting and training in righteousness, so that the servant of God may be thoroughly equipped for every good work" (2 Tim 3:16–17).

Helpful Sources:

Confession of Faith (1995), Article 4

Global Anabaptists, #4

What We Believe Together, 73–94

Claiming Faith, session 4

New City, 89–90

Presbyterian Q/A, 11–17

Suggested Practices:

Create a Bible reading challenge.

Suggested Hymns/Songs:

Thy word

Holy Spirit

Standing on the promises

Wonderful words of life

Holy Spirit rain down

How firm a foundation

B/G: I'm Using My Bible as a Roadmap

Call to Worship:

L: We gather today to worship the Lord our God.

SCRIPTURE

P: Lord Jesus, come among us. Fill our hearts with joy.

L: We gather today to hear God's Word for our lives

P: O Lord our God, speak to us through your Word in Scripture.

L: We gather together to give thanks, to learn God's Way, and find peace.

All: This is the day the Lord has made. Let us rejoice and be glad in it.

Confession and Absolution:

L: God calls us through his Holy Spirit and scripture to confess our sin.

P: O Lord, our God, you are holy, and you call us to be holy. We have not fulfilled our promise to follow you wholly.

[Moment for silent confession]

L: Lord, you set us aside for holy work.

P: Please forgive us for this week's failure to follow you fully Help us to rise to the challenge of making your Way our keenest desire. Grow our desire to know your Word.

L: The Lord has promised to forgive us our sin as we confess them. We are free to walk in his Way and not be embarrassed to speak openly and honestly with our God.

Offering Prayer:

Thank you, Lord Jesus, for your Word through your Spirit and scripture. Thank you, Lord God, for the gift of hope. We thank you for all your good gifts. Help us be generous, just as generous as you are with us. Amen.

Benediction:

May you find guidance, encouragement, hope, and peace as you read scripture. And now, the Lord bless you and keep you; the Lord make his face to shine upon you, and be gracious to you; the Lord lift up his countenance upon you, and give you peace. Amen.

11
God's Church

Introduction:

There is thought in song that "I am the church, you are the church, we are the church together," and that is correct. But it is not ours in the sense of ownership. It is God's: for the working of his Kingdom come. We do well when we allow the Holy Spirit to guide and direct our thinking and actions rather than hold too closely to tradition.

Theme:

The Church is God's tool for redeeming the World and ushering in "Thy Kingdom come."

Scripture:

Isaiah 2:1–5

Psalm 103

Ephesians 4:1–16 / 1 Corinthians 12:12–27

Matthew 6:9–13; 28:18–20; 18:15–20

Preaching Points:

The Church is made up of all believers.

TEACHING TENETS OF FAITH IN WORSHIP

We are faithful as we obey the Holy Spirit's lead to speak and serve.

We are called to proclaim God's Good News.

Our personal gifting of talents is for use in the Kingdom.

Unity within the Church is evidence of Christ's presence and his love within us.

Church discipline is needed to maintain righteousness for God's service.

Helpful Sources:

Confession of Faith (1995), Articles 9, 14

Global Anabaptists, #3, #4, #5, #6 & #7

Claiming Faith, session 5

Making Disciples, sessions 8 & 9

Heidelberg Catechism 91

What We Believe Together, 115–128, 129–154

New City, 100–101

Presbyterian Q/A, 63–66

Suggested Practices:

Give an assignment for the week to ponder what we are called to think and do to be faithful as part of God's Church.

Suggested Hymns/Songs:

The church's one foundation

Go ye into all the world

All glory, laud, and honor

All people that on earth do dwell

GOD'S CHURCH

We are God's people

In Christ there is no east or west

B/G: Working On a Building

B/G: [Do you know the] Father, Son, and Holy Ghost

Call to Worship:

L: Come, people of God. You are the Church.

P: We come to worship the One that calls us to serve.

L: Come, people of God. You are called to usher in the Kingdom of God.

P: We come. Equip us Spirit of Christ for greater faithfulness and service.

Confession and Absolution:

L: Let us prepare our hearts to receive God's Word. Sin distorts us. Sin distorts the Church. Sin keeps us from knowing God fully.

P: O Lord, our God, we have sinned, and our sin causes us to hide from you.

L: Let us confess our sins in silence.

[Moment for silent confession]

L: People of God, there is no reason to hide from God. Your sins are washed away. Work in the Church, with God's leading, to draw others to Christ.

All: Thanks be to God. We praise you, good and merciful Father, Son, and Holy Spirit. We thank you for your unending love. Help us to serve you faithfully. Amen.

TEACHING TENETS OF FAITH IN WORSHIP

Offering Prayer:

Lord, you have called us into service. We are part of your heavenly kingdom's hands and feet. Help us, we pray, to be faithful with our gifts of time, health, talent, and money for your Kingdom come, Lord Jesus. Amen.

Benediction:

It is time, people of God, to go into the world. Carry with you your faith. Carry with you your commission to be God's faithful people. And may you always know God's presence in your life and work. Amen.

12

The Commands-1

Introduction:

Scripture "is full of commands." God would not have us be ignorant of what pleases God. One may think of the commands being held in the Pentateuch, the Law, the first five books of the Bible; yet God's guidance and commands are throughout. Many Christians might think that the Law no longer holds sway upon Christians because we have Christ and the Holy Spirit to guide and direct us. Jesus said, "Do not think that I have come to abolish the law or the prophets; I have come not to abolish but to fulfill" (Matt 5:17). It is well that we learn the intent of God's law so that we can please God with our godly living.

Theme:

God's Commandments call us to righteousness/holiness.

Scripture:

Exodus 20 / Deuteronomy 5

Psalm 119:1-8

Hebrews 3

Matthew 5:18-20

Teaching Tenets of Faith in Worship

Preaching Points:

God calls his people to worship One God and follow God into righteousness.

Helpful Sources:

Global Anabaptists, #4

God's Story, ch. 2

Heidelberg Catechism, #92–115

New City, 22–39, and 42–43

Luther's Small Catechism, Part I–The Ten Commandments

Presbyterian Q/A, 89–90

Suggested Practices:

Encourage listeners to read either Exodus 20 or Deuteronomy 5 during the week and meditate upon their meaning for life. Why were those ten commands important?

Suggested Hymns/Songs:

A charge to keep I have

Teach me thy way O Lord

Holy, holy, holy

Take my life and let it be

Take time to be holy

O come, O come, Emmanuel

B/G: I'm Using My Bible as A Roadmap

B/G: Farther Along

B/G: I Am A Pilgrim

Call to Worship:

> L: We are called to love the Lord our God with heart, mind, and soul.
>
> P: We come, dear Lord God, to worship you only.
>
> L: Lead us Eternal Father, Son, and Holy Spirit.
>
> P: Lead us into righteousness by your Word. Fill our hearts with keen desire to follow and serve you all the days of our lives.

Confession and Absolution:

> L: People of God, we have not perfectly followed God's Law.
>
> P: We have not.
>
> L: In many ways we show that our hearts are not devoted to the Lord.
>
> P: Our hearts are bent on pleasing ourselves.
>
> *All: Please forgive us, Lord.*
>
> L: Let us confess our sins to the Lord God Almighty.
>
> [Moment for silent confession]
>
> L: People of God, our Lord is merciful and just to forgive us all our sins. We are called to live life boldly, remembering to confess our sins.
>
> *All: Thanks be to God who forgives us our sin and leads us into righteousness. Amen.*

Offering Prayer:

> O Lord, our God, please accept these offerings from us. You have given us everything we own, possess, and use. Help us remember—and be thankful. Lord, you have said you desire

us to be holy. Help us aspire to be holy as you are holy. We praise you and thank you in Jesus' name. Amen.

Benediction:

God's Law is meant for our salvation. It is meant to lead us into holiness. God calls us to be a holy, called out people. Let us walk into our living with true desire to be holy. Go in the name of the Father, Son, and Holy Spirit, knowing that God loves you. Amen.

13
The Commands–2

Introduction:

When asked about the greatest command Jesus replied, " . . . The first is, 'Hear, O Israel: the Lord our God, the Lord is one; you shall love the Lord your God with all your heart, and with all your soul, and with all your mind, and with all your strength.' The second is this, 'You shall love your neighbor as yourself.' There is no other commandment greater than these" (Mark 12:29–31). There is great simplicity in Jesus' summary. Stripped away are the technicalities that arise in people's minds about the Commandments, save one: "Who is my neighbor?" There too Jesus had an answer that stripped away technicalities that would limit our love.

Theme:

The simplicity of Christ's commands calls us to love God and our neighbors.

Scripture:

Isaiah 1:10–17 / Micah 6:8

Psalm 119:9–16

Romans 13:9

Matthew 22:34–40 / Luke 10:25–28 / Mark 12:28–24

TEACHING TENETS OF FAITH IN WORSHIP

Preaching Point:

God demands that our righteousness be practiced in love to one another.

Helpful Sources:

Confession of Faith (1995), Articles 17, 20, 22

Global Anabaptists, #4

God's Story, ch. 4

Presbyterian Q/A, 89

Luther's Small Catechism, Supplementary Parts, Table of Duties, Christians in General

Suggested Practices:

Encourage listeners to meditate during the week upon the radical nature of loving neighbors and enemies.

Suggested Hymns/Songs:

Footsteps of Jesus

Where he leads me

May the mind of Christ our Savior

Teach me thy way O Lord

Softly and tenderly .

Amazing grace

B/G: Just a Closer Walk With Thee

B/G: Purple Robe

Call to Worship:

L: Come to worship the King.

P: We come to worship Father, Son, and Holy Spirit by whom we are made whole.

L: Come and find hope in the Law through Jesus Christ.

P: We come. May the mind of Christ our Savior live in us. Amen.

Confession and Absolution:

L: People of God, Jesus Christ came to show us the way to please God. We fall short of his calling.

P: We have indeed fallen short. We have sinned against God by not following Christ. Please forgive us Lord. Fill us with your Holy Spirit and help us to follow you.

[Moment for silent confession]

L: Lift up your hearts. Our Lord sent his Son Jesus Christ to save us. In him we are not condemned.

All: Praise God Almighty who lifts us through the work of Jesus Christ. Amen.

Offering Prayer:

Dear Lord God, you have given us life and health and daily food. We thank you. Please help grow our hearts in thankfulness. We offer these gifts as a portion of your bounty in thanks. We thank you Lord Jesus Christ. Amen.

Benediction:

Go now, people of God. The heavy burden of Law has been lifted through the work of Jesus Christ. Go now and practice the Way of God—in Creation and with the people you find all around you. We are Christ's disciples as we love God and our neighbors. It is God's Way. May you find encouragement all through the week as you recall his great love. Amen.

14

Our Lord's Prayer

Introduction:

Jesus' prayer for us does not follow the ACTS formula put forward by religious preachers of the 20th century: adoration, confession, thanksgiving, and supplication. Rather, the Lord's Prayer dives into what we might view as Christ's demand for our holy living. We are called to honor God, ask for our needs, and participate in God's Kingdom Come through our practice of forgiving. Matthew's gospel delivers the prayer with Jesus' post script warning: "For if you forgive others their trespasses, your heavenly Father will also forgive you; but if you do not forgive others, neither will your Father forgive your trespasses" (Matt 6:14–15).

Theme:

God's will for us is found in the Lord's Prayer.

Scripture:

Proverbs 15:28–30

Psalm 119:17–24

Ephesians 3:14–21

Matthew 6:5–15 / Luke 11:1–13

Preaching Point:

    The Lord's Prayer teaches us how to live and pray.

Helpful Sources:

    Luther's Small Catechism, Part III

    Global Anabaptists, #2 & #7

    What We Believe Together, 41–42, 51–52, 104–105

Suggested Practice:

    Encourage listeners to meditate upon the Lord's Prayer during the week. What aspects seem new? In what aspects do you need the most help?

Suggested Hymns/Songs:

    The Lord's prayer

    Day by day

    If my people's hearts be humbled

    Jesus loves the little children

    Jesus loves me this I know

    Amazing grace

    B/G: O Healing River

    B/G: Just a Closer Walk With Thee

Call to Worship:

    L: We gather to worship the King.

    P: We gather to worship the One who is All in All.

    L: The Lord our God calls us to worship and to forgive.

P: We come to worship the King and to practice the forgiveness that God showers upon us.

Confession and Absolution:

L: People of God, if there are things in your heart that you need to forgive others, now is the time to reflect and forgive.

P: Dear Lord, focus our thinking upon those people and actions that we need to forgive. Free us from our grudges and hard hearts.

[Moment for reflection]

L: To forgive others is the hard work that true believers are called to do.

P: Help us Lord. Don't let us harden our hearts to others—and in doing so to harden our hearts to you. Please forgive us our sins as we forgive those who sin against us.

[Moment for silent confession]

L: People of God, may you desire to freely do the hard work of forgiving others. Jesus promises to forgive us as we do so.

All: Help us, Lord Jesus. Amen.

Offering Prayer:

Dear Lord, you have given us everything we own, and possess, and use. Thank you. Please accept these offered gifts from us now, and help us forgive others even as you forgive us. Amen.

Benediction:

It is time now, people of God, to bless the world. As you find grudges within you towards people and God, may you willingly forgive them. It is in your forgiving that you will be freed. Go now; bless the world. Amen.

15

Confession

Introduction:

We are invited into God's holy presence to speak freely. We are invited to confess/acknowledge the sin in our lives, and seek help from the One who truly loves us. Our practiced pride often gets in the way of confession, either from the embarrassment of facing sin head-on or foolishly thinking if we do not mention certain things then they do not exist! Indeed, God knows all things. It is so much better that we speak freely, open our mind and heart to our Creator, and seek his help. Until we do that, we are slaves of the sinful things we have done. Confession cleans the tally sheet, lifts the heavy burden from our souls of hiding, and brings us hope. As King David found, he still faced consequences among people, but his spirit was freed to love and hope anew.

Theme:

God restores us to fellowship as we confess our sin.

Scripture:

Genesis 3:1–8, 12, 13

Psalm 32:4–6; 51:1–19

1 John 1:8–10 / James 5:15–16

Mark 1:1–8

TEACHING TENETS OF FAITH IN WORSHIP

Preaching Points:

Adam & Eve sinned; as a result they hid from God.

Our sin causes us to shrink from a Holy God.

As we confess our sins, God is merciful and just to forgive us.

Helpful Sources:

Confession of Faith (1995), Article 7

Global Anabaptists, #3

New City, 74–75

Luther's Small Catechism, Intermediate Part of Confession

Presbyterian Q/A, 72–73

Suggested Practice:

Conduct corporate confession in worship.

Suggested Hymns/Songs:

Come, thou fount of every blessing

Cleanse me (Ellers or Maori)

I lay my sins on Jesus

If my people's hearts are humbled

Turn your eyes upon Jesus

Whiter than snow

B/G: Peter Was a Fireball

B/G: Did Trouble Me

Call to Worship:

L: Come, people of God. Come and worship.

P: We come to worship the Lord.

L: Come, people of God. Come and worship the One who knows us.

P: We come to the One that knows us through and through.

Confession and Absolution:

L: Dear Lord . . .

All: We confess that our outward lives miss your mark of holiness. We confess that our thoughts dwell on the unholy. Please forgive us.

L: Though we strive to know you and follow your ways . . .

All: We confess that we have sinned against you by what we have done and by what we have left undone. Please forgive us.

[Moment for silent confession]

L: People of God, be assured that as we confess our sins, the Lord our God is merciful and just to forgive us all our sin. Walk now in the wholeness of beauty, seeking God's face and following God's Way.

All: Praise be to God.

Offering Prayer:

We praise you and thank you, Lord, for all your gifts so freely given—life and health and shelter and daily food. Help us, Lord Jesus, to open our hearts to others—just as wide as you have given those things to us. Amen.

Benediction:

Go into the world knowing that you may call upon the Lord every moment of your life. God is willing to know you, and lead you into beauty and love. You are not alone. In fact, you never were alone. Amen.

16

Reform to Follow Christ

Introduction:

> The Reformation is said to have begun in 1517 when Luther posted his "Ninety-five Theses" on the door of the Wittenberg Chapel. In truth there were motions of reforming the Church well before that time. Though some say the Reformation ended in the mid-17th century, there is much to say that with every theological discussion or schism, the Church is being reformed. God desires that all through our individual lives we be formed ever closer to the image of Jesus Christ. Thus, in our faithfulness to that calling, reformation continues.

Theme:

> The Church was and is in need of reformation to follow Christ.

Scripture:

> Exodus 20:1–3 / Deuteronomy 10:12–22
>
> Psalm 100
>
> 1 John 2:7–4:21 / James 1–3
>
> Matthew 5–7 / John 1:1–18

Preaching Points:

Josiah's reform in Judah

Nehemiah's reforms in reestablishing Jerusalem

The Church and the period of the Reformation

Anabaptist-Mennonite distinctives include:

- Jesus Christ is the lens to understand all scripture;
- Separation of church and state;
- Humankind is called to live in peace;
- The Mission of God is to reconcile the world to God; and
- Christ calls us to live humbly, serve one another, and tend Creation daily.

Helpful Sources:

God's Story, ch. 9

What We Believe Together, 153–161

Adventures,[1] all

Presbyterian Q/A, 3–4

Suggested Practices:

Give an assignment for the week to ponder what reforming is needed in our hearts and living to better reflect Jesus Christ? (Don't engage in finger pointing at other people, but consider our own need for reformation.)

Suggested Hymns/Songs:

We are the church

I love thy Kingdom, Lord

---

1. Grieser and Duerksen, *Adventures With the Anabaptists*, all.

Servant Song (Will you help me be your servant?)

We are God's people

We come, O Christ, to you

Holy, holy, holy

B/G: Amazing Grace

B/G: He's Right on Time

B/G: I'm Using My Bible as A Roadmap

Call to Worship:

L: Come, people of God, come to worship the Lord our God.

P: We come to worship our Creator and Sustainer.

L: Come, people of God, and find rest for your souls.

P: Thank you, Lord Jesus, for welcoming us into your presence.

Confession and Absolution:

L: God welcomes us into his presence, yet in so many ways we hide from God as did our forbearers, Adam and Eve. It is sin that causes us to hide.

P: Dear Lord Jesus, we admit that sin creeps into our lives. Help us to ponder and confess our sins. We desire to be cleansed and whole.

L: Let us confess our sins.

[Moment for silent confession]

L: People of God, rejoice in the news that God will not remember our sin as we humbly confess.

P: Praise God, the One who forgives us our sin and transgression! Help us, Lord Jesus, to forget old habits of sin and come out of hiding from you. You are the One that loves us.

All: Thank you, Lord Jesus.

Offering Prayer:

O Lord our God, you have given us everything we possess in time, health, and possessions. You are the One that brings hope to all humankind. Help us to honor you with our lives, and with these offerings. Bless the Church as we bless you with our devotion. Amen.

Benediction:

Let your integrity of faith and living be so evident to a watching world that they are drawn to our Lord Jesus Christ. Go in faith, hope, and love. Serve the Lord. He has promised to be with you always. Amen.

17

Discerning the Way

Introduction:

All through life to be faithful we discern God's Way forward for our individual and corporate lives. We are not free to rely on tradition alone, for God is not dead but lives and calls us to respond to God's movement in human history. We have been given tools for discernment via Scripture, God's Holy Spirit, and yes, tradition. We need the tools to help us find God's Way.

Themes:

God desires our faithful obedience.

God desires we distinguish true Christian faith from cults.

Scripture:

1 Kings 3:5–12 / 2 Kings 22:14–20

Psalm 27 / Proverbs 15:14

Acts 2:22–39 / 1 John 4:1–3 / 2 John 4–11

John 14:1–14 / Matthew 28:16–20

Preaching Points:

Beware: Satan comes as an angel of light.

Father, Son, and Holy Spirit are to be praised as One God.

Faith in Jesus Christ and obeying his commands is our pathway to life.

Practical advice for spiritual discernment.

Helpful Sources:

What We Believe Together, all

Adventures, all

Christianity, Cults & Religions[1]

Suggested Practices:

Give an assignment for the week to pray for God's leading in a specific area of life.

Suggested Hymns/Songs:

Holy, holy, holy

All hail the power of Jesus' name

At the name of Jesus

Crown him with many crowns

Fairest Lord Jesus

Jesus, thy blood and righteousness

B/G: Good News

B/G: What a Friend We Have in Jesus

B/G: Amazing Grace

---

1. Carden, ed., *Christianity, Cults, & Religions*, all.

Call to Worship:

>L: We are called into the presence of the Lord.

>P: We come to praise the Lord our God.

>L: Come, let us speak of whom we worship.

>P: It is God we worship: Father, Son, and Holy Ghost.

Confession and Absolution:

>L: The world presents many ways; all of them false gods. None of them glorify and follow the true God. We become confused and follow false ways.

>P: Forgive us Lord for letting our eyes stray. Show us the error of our ways.

>[Moment for silent confession]

>L: You are the called of God. As you confess your sins the Lord is merciful and just to forgive you of all sin. May we resolve to follow God truly and seek God's help.

>P: Dear Lord, please help us discern your ways, acknowledge your Word, and follow you with integrity. We praise your name, Lord Jesus. Amen.

Offering Prayer:

>God calls us to faithful lives of integrity, holding fast to Christ Jesus. Let us open our hearts in thanksgiving to God and hospitality to all people. Amen.

Benediction:

>Go now into the world recognizing we are called out by God to come out from the world, called to be faithful to the Lord Jesus Christ, acknowledging God's ownership upon our lives. Go in peace. Serve the Lord.

18

Communion and Washing Feet

Introduction:

Believers have been given two memorials to help them remember Christ's way. Three gospels recall Jesus' last supper with the Twelve. One gospel does not mention detail of that supper but focuses on Jesus washing the Twelve's feet. It is important for us to consider those very different practices. What do they signify? How can we make them vital after so many years of repeated practice? In both cases, Jesus called on believers to practice them and remember.

Theme:

Jesus set forth two practices to remember him by and to practice his way.

Scripture:

Exodus 20:18–21

Psalm 104:1, 14–16

1 Corinthians 11:17–29

Matthew 26:17–30 / Mark 14:12–26 / Luke 22:7–20 / John 6:35, 48, 51; John 13:1–17 / Matthew 20:20–28

TEACHING TENETS OF FAITH IN WORSHIP

Preaching Points:

Jesus freely shared his body and blood with all the disciples, both faithful and unfaithful.

Jesus provided practices of communion and footwashing for us to remember him.

Communion reminds us of our dependence upon the Lord Jesus Christ for salvation; footwashing reminds us of Jesus' command to serve others, for surely the last shall be first and the first shall be last.

Helpful Sources:

Confession of Faith (1995), Articles 12, 13

Global Anabaptists, #6

God's Story, ch. 7

Claiming Faith, session 6

Heidelberg Catechism, #66, 75–82

New City, 91–92, 96–99

Presbyterian Q/A, 83–86

Luther's Small Catechism, Part V – The Sacrament of the Altar or The Lord's Supper

Suggested Practices:

Conduct Communion (Lord's Supper) during worship

Conduct foot washing during worship

Suggested Hymns/Songs:

Let us break bread together on our knees

Will you let me be your servant?

COMMUNION AND WASHING FEET

Break thou the Bread of Life

May the mind of Christ, my Savior

Let your heart be broken

Come all Christians be committed

B/G: Amazing Grace

B/G: Stumbling Blocks

Call to Worship:

L: We are invited into God's presence.

P: We come with thanksgiving.

L: We are invited to Christ's table.

P: We come with thanksgiving.

L: We are commanded to learn and do Christ's Way.

P: We look to God's grace to fill us with fear and hope.

Confession and Absolution:

L: As we approach the table of our Lord Jesus Christ, it is right and pleasing to God that we confess our sins.

P: Dear Lord, we come humbly to you.

L: Though we endeavor to be true believers and practitioners of God's Word in Jesus Christ, we fall into sin.

P: Lord Jesus, please help us examine our lives. Help us to root out all sin that enslaves us to Satan.

[Moment for silent confession]

L: God is merciful and just. God will forgive us as we confess our sins.

All: Thanks be to God, the eternal One in Three, Father, Son, and Holy Spirit. Amen.

Offering Prayer:

Dear Lord, you gave your body and blood in the form of bread and wine to the disciples. Help us to live in thankfulness for your wonderful gift of love to us. You also commanded us to love our neighbors, to wash people's feet, and serve them as we can. Help us to live lives that honor you and serve other people. We thank you now for all good gifts that you have given us. Please accept our offerings and bless them. Amen.

Benediction:

People of God, we have been given things to remember about our Lord Jesus Christ. He gave us life, and he calls us to give life-giving gifts to the people around us near and far. Go now in the service of our Lord Jesus Christ knowing that he is with you—even to the end of the age. Amen.

19

God's Gifted People

Introduction:

Evangelists, prophets, preachers, and teachers are specifically mentioned as gifts for the betterment of the Church, but the Apostle Paul was clear that those were not the only gifts of importance. All believers have God-given talents, skills, and abilities for the good of the Church. We each are to use them for his Kingdom come.

Theme:

Each person has God-given talents to use for God's Kingdom.

Scripture:

Numbers 11:24–30

Psalm 133

Romans 12 / 1 Corinthians 12 / Acts 10:45–48

Mark 13:11

Preaching Points:

God gives believers certain gifts to contribute to the community of faith.

TEACHING TENETS OF FAITH IN WORSHIP

Our spiritual gifting is meant to be practical.

Our spiritual gifting may puff our ego; watch out!

Helpful Sources:

Confession of Faith (1995), Articles 6 & 15

Global Anabaptists, #3, #4, #5, #6 & #7

God's Story, ch. 2, 7 & 8

Making Disciples, sessions 8 & 9

Claiming Faith, session 1 and 7

Heidelberg Catechism, #1–4, 86, 88–91

New City, 10–11, 16–17, 20–21, 76–77

Presbyterian Q/A, 37–44, 48–49, 71–72, 77–78

Suggested Practices:

Give an assignment for the week to ponder our own specific gifting. How have those gifts been used for the Kingdom? Give thanks.

Suggested Hymns/Songs:

We are God's people

We are one in the Spirit (They'll Know We are Christians by Our Love)

Take my life and let it be

A charge to keep I have

Come, all Christians, be committed

Freely, freely

B/G: Use Your Shield

B/G: There's No Better Time Than Now

Call to Worship:

L: Come, servants of God.

P: We come to worship the King.

L: Come, servants of God. Let us worship God the Father, Son, and Holy Spirit.

P: It is right to give God thanks and praise.

Confession and Absolution:

L: We are invited to come before God to confess our sins. Let us do so that we may be restored into fellowship and service to God.

P: We have fallen short of God's glory and righteousness. We confess that we have made our plans first and asked God's blessing afterwards. Lord, you called us to be your servant people yet we have used our gifts for our own joy and have not freely shared them with Creation and your people. Dear Lord, our God, please hear our confessions.

[Moment for silent confession]

L: O Lord, please hear our confessions.

P: Please forgive us and lead us forward into the light. Help us to serve you willingly, fully, and with great joy.

L: Our Lord is merciful and just, and will forgive us as we confess our sin.

All: *Praise be to God!*

Offering Prayer:

Lord God, you created us for fellowship and faithful service. You seek our love and openhearted, open-handed stewardship of your Creation. Please help us in our tasks, Lord. Help us with our hearts. You are the One that can create in us true hearts. We offer you now a part of what you first gave us. Help us be generous with our lives, our time, our talents, and the wealth we now possess. Thank you, generous Father. Amen.

Benediction:

May the Lord bless you and keep you as you serve God's people and Creation by your gifting—in God's blessed name. Amen.

20
Called Out of the World

Introduction:

Humankind forms cultures of tastes, skillsets, expectations, and moral and ethical mores. Cultures vary widely around the world. We most often believe that our own culture is superior to others merely because we know our own the best. What is sadly true of all cultures is that humankind's sin-nature permeates them. Scripture refers to cultures as "the world." God calls believers "out of the world" and "be Holy for I the Lord am Holy" (Lev 11:45).

Themes:

Faithful believers are in many ways different from the world.

The world will notice the difference of faithful believers; that will bring both inquisitiveness and persecution.

Scripture:

Leviticus 11:45 / Proverbs 9

Psalm 5

Romans 12:1–2

John 15:18–20; 17:15–17

Preaching Points:

We are called to be holy even as God is Holy.

If no one is offended by our godly presence, we fit into the world too well.

They will know us by our love and peace.

Helpful Sources:

Confession of Faith (1995), Articles 23, 24

Global Anabaptists, #5

God's Story, ch. 7 & 8

Claiming Faith, sessions 8, 9 & 10

Making Disciples, sessions 8 & 9

New City, 76–77

Presbyterian Q/A, 93–94

Suggested Practices:

Create a moment for bringing slips of paper to the front that describe how we pledge to be different from the world (our culture).

Suggested Hymns/Songs:

We are one in the Spirit (They'll Know We Are Christians by Our Love)

Am I a soldier of the cross?

Day by day

May the love

Let the peace of Christ rule in your heart

Will you let me be your servant?

B/G: I Am a Pilgrim

B/G: Just a Closer Walk

B/G: Wasted Years

B/G: He Took Your Place

Call to Worship:

L: You are called and welcomed to worship the Lord your God.

P: Come, let us praise the Lord. May our thoughts and actions be acceptable to our Righteous King.

L: We are called to find ourselves in God's peace.

P: We are called up and out. We are called to be holy. We are called out of the world. May our words and deeds be honorable and right before the Lord.

Confession and Absolution:

L: The world beckons us. In many ways we fit into the world all too well.

P: O Lord, our God, please forgive us for being afraid to be like you. Forgive us for desiring to fit into the world.

L: Life has a way of presenting attractive idols that demand our time.

P: We ask God to forgive us for placing our hope and trust and devotion to things other than God.

L: The world offers pleasures and fellowships that unfit us for God's service.

P: O Lord, our God, please forgive us for desiring the things of this world instead of fitting ourselves for your service.

L: Assembled people, do you disavow your idolatrous hope in money, work, position, and personal and military strength?

P: We do. Help us, Lord Jesus, to be true to our vow.

[Moment for silent confession]

L: People of God, as the called-out ones, your security is in Christ. Make good on your pledge of single-minded devotion to God.

All: May we accept God's forgiveness and walk with integrity of faith and life. Help us, Lord Jesus Christ, to be devoted to you only. Amen.

Offering Prayer:

O Lord, our God, you call us out of the world to be perfect, righteous, and holy, even as you are perfect, righteous, and holy. We stand amazed at your calling. Help us to faithfully walk in your ways, being as wholly in love with Creation as you are. Please accept our gifts for your service. Amen.

Benediction:

L: We are called out of the world to serve the Lord and all God's Creation.

P: May we strive to walk with integrity, joining our faith and our living in Jesus name. Amen.

L: Go. Serve the Lord with gladness knowing that Jesus Christ promised to be near you always, now and all through the week.

21

In Thanks—1: Open Hands

Introduction:

Thankfulness does not stand alone. True thankfulness to God is coupled with hearts that are open to love practically. Much of faithfulness is so coupled. Action is the required ingredient that indicates faith is real. Remembering who gives all good gifts is helpful in fighting the human urge to hold too tightly onto the things given us freely.

Theme:

Thankfulness for salvation gives believers big hearts.

Scripture:

Ezra 3:1–13 / 1 Chronicles 16:7–36

Psalm 148

2 Corinthians 9:6–15 / 1 Thessalonians 5:18

Mark 6:41

Preaching Points:

"Now he who supplies seed to the sower and bread for food will also supply and increase your store of seed and will enlarge the harvest of your righteousness" (2 Cor 9:10).

God loves a cheerful giver.

The people of God belong to God; they are not their own.

Helpful Sources:

Confession of Faith (1995), Article 21

Global Anabaptists, #5

Luther's Small Catechism, Part II–Creed, First Article – Of Creation

Suggested Practices:

Instead of passing offering plates during offering, have people come forward to give their offerings.

Suggested Hymns/Songs:

Come, ye thankful people, come

Count your blessings

For health and strength and daily food

We gather together to ask the Lord's blessing

God is so good

We give thee but thine own

B/G: There's No Better Time than Now to Praise the Lord

B/G: I Am Going to a City

Call to Worship:

L: Are we God's People?

P: Yes, we come as God's People to worship God in thankfulness.

L: As God's People you are not your own.

P: Our time and talent and resources are God's. Help us, Lord, to be faithful with what you give us. We praise your name. Amen.

Confession and Absolution:

L: As God's People, we are called to confess our sin.

P: Lord Jehovah Jireh, you are our Provider. Please forgive us for the times we held tightly onto the things you gave us instead of sharing them with those in need.

L: The people around us have many needs.

P: Please forgive us when we did not share with people in need—of our time, our talents, and our resources.

L: What do you lack?

P: There are things that we want, but what you have given us is excellent and good. Thank you for your providence. Please forgive us our fear and greed. You are good.

[Moment for silent confession]

L: Dear People of God, rest assured that as you confess your sin that God is merciful and just to forgive you all your sin.

All: Help us all, dear Lord, to have big hearts that share what you give us so freely. Thank you, Lord Jesus. Amen.

Offering Prayer:

We come before you, Lord Jehovah Jireh, to admit that everything we have comes from you. We admit that none of it is meant for our pleasure only but is to be shared to bless others. Please open our hearts and minds to share freely of what you give us, and to be as free with them as you were in giving them to us. We thank you and praise your name, Lord Jesus. Amen.

Benediction:

Go now, People of God, to help the world. We belong to the Lord. We have been given much, and it is intended to bless the whole world. Open your hearts this week; follow where God leads your heart. May you find wonderful, great joy as you share your time, talents, and resources—in Christ's name. Amen.

22

In Thanks—2: Stewardship

Introduction:

Believers in Jesus Christ are called to be stewards of Creation. All things and beings are precious in God's sight. "For God so loved the world that he sent his Son . . . " (John 3:16). With that as backdrop, even soil must not be treated as dirt. Stewardship, therefore, encompasses all things.

Theme:

We are called to be God's stewards of all God's creation.

Scripture:

Genesis 2:4b–15 / Isaiah 28:23–29 / Deuteronomy 10:12

Psalm 115

Colossians 4:2 / Acts 10:1–4

Matthew 6:1–24

Preaching Point:

Fear of the Lord causes us to protect and nurture all that God has made.

Helpful Sources:

Confession of Faith (1995), Article 21

Global Anabaptists, #5

Luther's Small Catechism, Part II–Creed, First Article—Of Creation

Suggested Practices:

Give an assignment for the week to ponder how God has already been calling us to help preserve his creation.

Suggested Hymns/Songs:

We are God's people

For the beauty of the earth

This is my Father's world

All creatures of our God and King

All things bright and beautiful

B/G: For God So Loved the World

B/G: O Healing River

B/G: Working on a Building

Call to Worship:

L: We come to worship the God of Creation.

P: It is right to give God thanks and praise!

L: The Lord God in Jesus Christ created all things.

P: We come to worship Christ and pledge to nurture what he made.

Confession and Absolution:

L: O Lord our God, we have not always been faithful in protecting what you created.

P: We confess that we have squandered portions of our time and talent in trivial pursuits. We confess that we have not consciously nurtured your Creation—not giving it the care it deserves.

L: We ask for your forgiveness.

[Moment for silent confession]

L: People of God, please know that as you confess your sins, God is faithful and just to forgive us our unrighteousness. Know, too, that we are not free to live in sin, but are called to change our ways and work for the good of God's Kingdom.

All: We thank you for your mercy. Please help us to be faithful stewards of your Creation. In Jesus Christ's name we pray. Amen.

Offering Prayer:

O Lord our God, you have given us time, talents, and possessions. Please help us to be open-handed with your gifts for the benefit of others and your Creation. Help us to be faithful stewards. Amen.

Benediction:

As you go into God's Creation, know that you have been given a job to tend the earth for our Lord. Go joyfully; be faithful and seek God's help in all your tasks. May the Lord bless you and keep you. The Lord make his face to shine upon you, and be gracious to you. The Lord lift up his countenance upon your and give you peace. Amen.

23

Justice with Peace

Introduction:

It is God's will that all people live in peace. The Hebrew word *shalom* has a meaning much broader than peace. It also encompasses justice, harmony, completeness, prosperity, tranquility, and more. Believers are called not only to seek shalom for themselves, but also for all people.

Themes:

God's will for believers is that they live in peace.

There is no peace if we are full of violence.

We must denunciate all forms of violence.

Scripture:

Amos 5:18–24 / Proverbs 14:30

Psalm 11

Galatians 5:22–26 / Romans 14:17, 15:13

Matthew 5:38–48 / John 14:23–31 / Luke 9:51–56

Preaching Points:

Attributes of God

Fruit of the Spirit

Generous hearts produce peace

Helpful Sources:

The Attributes of God, Volume 1

Confession of Faith (1995), Article 22

Global Anabaptists, #5 & #7

What We Believe Together, 95–98

God's Story, ch. 8

Claiming Faith, session 9

Suggested Practices:

Give an assignment for the week to ponder and identify the violence that is deep-seated in our thinking—about people and situations we face.

Suggested Hymns/Songs:

Let justice roll down

May the mind of Christ, my Savior

Cause me to come to thy river, O Lord

Peace, perfect peace

O happy day

Wonderful peace

B/G: On Heaven's Bright Shore

B/G: Just a Closer Walk

B/G: O Healing River

TEACHING TENETS OF FAITH IN WORSHIP

Call to Worship:

L: People of God, we are called to live in peace as we seek justice for all peoples.

P: We come to worship you, Lord God Almighty. Help us to desire your peace within us.

L: Come, find joy in the Lord who brings peace and hope for our lives.

P: We come.

Confession and Absolution:

L: Scripture tells us that prophets cry out for peace in times of trouble. "'Peace, peace,' they say."[1] Yet there is no peace without our willing participation.

P: Lord Jesus Christ, guide our thinking into the ways of peace and help us to desire it more than having our own way.

L: We have not worked faithfully toward peaceable ways in our lives.

P: We confess that we are bent on pleasing ourselves more than pleasing God.

[Moment for silent confession]

L: People of God, our Lord promised to lead us into the ways of peace, but we must willingly follow.

All: Help us, Spirit of God, to desire and practice your ways of peace and justice for all people.

L: Our Lord is merciful and just to forgive us our sin as we humbly confess. May we faithfully walk forward in peace.

All: Amen.

---

1. Jeremiah 6:14.

Offering Prayer:

O Lord our God, the prophet Micah told us, "He has shown you, O mortal, what is good. And what does the Lord require of you? To act justly and to love mercy and to walk humbly with your God."[2] Help us give you our just and merciful living as our best offering. Accept now these offerings as our token of promise. We praise and thank you for all you have given us, Lord Jesus Christ. Amen.

Benediction:

May the Lord bless you as you endeavor to walk forward in peace. May your walk be held blameless. May you be full of the quiet doings of peace, hope, and love. May the Lord bless you and keep you in the name of the Lord of Peace, Jesus Christ. Amen.

---

2. Micah 6:8.

24

What We Await

Introduction:

In the midst of living, the mundane fills our thinking, causing us to forget our ultimate future. Yet an end of "this world" is coming and there is a future that lies beyond. What has God told us about the future?

Theme:

Judgment and glorious worship of God are yet to come.

Scripture:

Exodus 6:1–8 / Deuteronomy 10:12–22 / Ezra 3:1–6

Psalm 150

Revelation 14:6–13, 20:11–15

Matthew 25:31–46

Preaching Points:

We will be judged for what we have done.

God knows the motives of our hearts.

Worship God only.

Helpful Sources:

Confession of Faith (1995), Article 24

God's Story, ch. 9

Presbyterian Q/A, 95–97, 100–101

Suggested Practices:

Give an assignment for the week to ponder what things Jesus Christ will praise us for doing and thinking. Ponder also what things Christ will Judge us for doing and thinking. Ask for forgiveness and help now to make needed changes in our lives.

Suggested Hymns/Songs:

Holy, holy, holy

All creatures of our God and King

Come, thou Almighty King

Joyful, joyful, we adore thee

To God be the glory

We gather together to sing the Lord's blessing

My Jesus, I love thee

There's something about that name

Thou art worthy

We will glorify

B/G: I am Going to a City

B/G: Heaven's Bright Shore

B/G: I am a Pilgrim

B/G: I'll Not be a Stranger

B/G: I'll Fly Away

TEACHING TENETS OF FAITH IN WORSHIP

B/G: Old Rugged Cross

B/G: When the Roll Is Called Up Yonder

Call to Worship:

L: Today we worship; tomorrow we meet in glory!

P: O Lord our God, we glorify your name above all things. You are the One that created all things. You are the One who will Judge the world and make all things right.

L: Come, Lord Jesus.

P: Today we worship; tomorrow we meet in glory!

Confession and Absolution:

L: One day all things will be made right. One day all peoples will be judged for their actions—both good and evil. Come, people of God, let us confess our sins and be made right in God's sight.

P: O Lord our God, we have sinned. We have not lived in love. We have forgotten to do the things you called us to do. Please forgive us.

[Moment for silent confession]

L: People of God, as we confess our sins the Lord our God is merciful and just to forgive us our sin.

P: Praise the Lord!

L: Walk with integrity, making your faith and your life as one thing.

All: Help us, Lord Jesus, to walk with integrity. Amen.

Offering Prayer:

Dear Lord, you are the giver of all good things. Help grow our thankfulness. Grow our hearts to willingly give to others what they need—that we may all praise your name. We offer these gifts in Jesus' name. Amen.

Benediction:

L: Today, we worship the Lord our God. Tomorrow we meet in glory to praise God forevermore!

P: O Lord our God, we glorify your name above all things.

L: Lord Jesus, help us to please you all the days of our lives—by the power of your name.

All: Come, Lord Jesus! Come in power. Heal our hearts and lead us in faith. Amen.

Epilogue—Why We Teach Tenets of Faith

The Bible is clear that God does not delight in humankind being left in the dark about God's self. We are invited to know God through Jesus Christ, the Commandments, and the Holy Spirit.[1] We are called to have fellowship with God for God's benefit and that we might be set free from the tyranny of sin.[2] Additionally, we are not free to appropriate what we know of the LORD God in combination with other gods and idols we may fancy. We are called to recognize and worship the LORD God Almighty only.[3] Church leaders are called upon to utilize scripture, instruction, correction, and exhortation to teach believers and seekers in the way of Christ and to correct wrong thinking that becomes apparent.[4] We will need to unwrap these words to understand the theological framework and purpose of our work.

Called to Know God

We are invited and called to know God. That is apparent in the history of God's walk with humanity, in God's presentation of religious law throughout scripture, and in denominational faith statements. Genesis 1:27–28 depicts our early relationship with

1. Exod 20, Deut 4:35, Ps 34:8, and John 14:7.
2. Col 1:16, Rev 4:11.
3. Deut 4:2, 5:7–8.
4. Matt 28:18–20, 2 Tim 3:16, 1 Cor 12:27–30.

God. In that first mention of our relationship with God we learn that God spoke to humanity, blessed them, and gave them a task. It is a direct, one-on-one relationship, where humankind is given purpose and meaning.

> "So God created humankind in his image, in the image of God he created them; male and female he created them. God blessed them, and God said to them, "Be fruitful and multiply, and fill the earth and subdue it; and have dominion over the fish of the sea and over the birds of the air and over every living thing that moves upon the earth." (Gen 1:27–28 NRSV)[5]

Additional insight about our relationship with God is given in the second Creation account. Here we see our commissioned work, delegated authority, and even a hint at a playful relationship!

> "The LORD God took the man and put him in the Garden of Eden to work it and take care of it . . . Now the LORD God had formed out of the ground all the wild animals and all the birds in the sky. He brought them to the man to see what he would name them; and whatever the man called each living creature, that was its name." (Gen 2:15, 19)

While God did all the work of Creation, and created the fish, birds, and animals, God brought the living creatures to humanity to name, and "whatever the man called each living creature, that was its name[!]" From the beginning there was a close, appreciative relationship, where God trusted humanity to do our best, where God did not overrule our decisions, and where humanity worked in partnership in blessing what God had done—for surely, to name something is to acknowledge it, bless it, and give it importance. Indeed, philosophers believe that to name something is to give it existence; once named, a creature cannot be denied its place in reality.[6] Thus, God playfully gave humanity a key role in the act of

---

5. All quoted scripture is New International Version (NIV) unless, as with this, otherwise cited.

6. Jager, *The Development of Bertrand Russell's Philosophy*, 257, accessed December 16, 2017, https://books.google.com/books?id=QYoqD-27T50C&

TEACHING TENETS OF FAITH IN WORSHIP

Creation itself. We continue that work as we learn more about the world, naming newfound creatures, cosmic entities, and processes. As an aside, we are faithful to God's commission as we tend and preserve them as well.

There was a time of wonderful fellowship between humankind and God as evidenced by God's tender desire to create a "helper as . . . partner" for Adam (Gen 2:20) and in the daily walks "in the cool of a day" that God devoted to be with mankind (Gen 3:8–9). After humankind's fall into disobedience and sin, however, humanity became blinded to the existence, power, and delight of God. God knows we do not now naturally look to God. Our hearts need help to seek and know God. The prophet says of God, "I will give them a heart to know me, that I am the Lord. They will be my people, and I will be their God, for they will return to me with all their heart" (Jer 24:7). Dozens of times in scripture God finds ways to convince us that the Lord is God.

Relationship and witness of God's mighty acts are early means to convince us. In Exodus 6:7 God says, "I will take you as my own people, and I will be your God. Then you will know that I am the Lord your God, who brought you out from under the yoke of the Egyptians." God's reasoning appears to be that in the relationship itself and in the witness of the Lord's mighty acts the people would come to know God. Merely witnessing God's mighty acts was also intended as means to such knowledge. God reasoned that Pharaoh and the Egyptians would know God by their witness of the plagues against them (Exod 7:5). To hear God's prophets foretell an event and then to witness fulfillment leads to knowing. As with the Egyptians, so it was with unfaithful people of Israel. The prophet said, "Your people will fall slain among you, and you will know that I am the Lord" (Ezek 6:7). Similar statements to the effect that relationship and/or witness cause knowing, whether of blessings or punishments, are replete in scripture. Jesus speaks in

---

pg=PA257&lpg=PA257&dq=to+name+something&source=bl&ots=HZeoh5yCOz&sig=RXUdyMLSDiYde04pU18P5uc0JZg&hl=en&sa=X&ved=0ahUKEwi9z9Go5o7YAhXGKyYKHX3KBFo4ChDoAQg9MAQ#v=onepage&q=to%20name%20something&f=false.

EPILOGUE—WHY WE TEACH TENETS OF FAITH

the same vein: " . . . When you have lifted up the Son of Man, then you will know that I am he and that I do nothing on my own but speak just what the Father has taught me" (John 8:28).

God instituted religious rites and encouragement to tell family stories of God's mighty acts so that future generations would know the LORD. An example is the instruction regarding the Festival of Tabernacles: "Live in temporary shelters for seven days: All native-born Israelites are to live in such shelters so your descendants will know that I had the Israelites live in temporary shelters when I brought them out of Egypt. I am the LORD your God" (Lev 23:42–44). God tells us that faithfully remembering what we have seen and experienced is a means to the end of knowing God. Moses spoke to Joshua, "You know with all your heart and soul that not one of all the good promises the LORD your God gave you has failed" (Josh 23:14b).

God encourages quiet times, reasoning that if we take moments of our lives to be quiet, our souls will remember and know God better. In Psalm 46:10a the psalmist says, "Be still, and know that I am God."

God's Word and Holy Spirit witness to us that God is LORD of all. God's teaching has always been passed along by the faithful. In Deuteronomy we learn:

> "Moses came with Joshua son of Nun and spoke all the words of this song in the hearing of the people. When Moses finished reciting all these words to all Israel, he said to them, 'Take to heart all the words I have solemnly declared to you this day, so that you may command your children to obey carefully all the words of this law. They are not just idle words for you—they are your life. By them you will live long in the land you are crossing the Jordan to possess.'" (32:44–47)

We learn too that God's written word is intended to teach us of God: "All Scripture is God-breathed and is useful for teaching, rebuking, correcting and training in righteousness" (2 Tim 3:16).

It is the Holy Spirit that bears witness to the truth we hear. The Holy Spirit also helps us understand what we read. The apostle said, "This is the one who came by water and blood—Jesus Christ. He did not come by water only, but by water and blood. And it is the Spirit who testifies, because the Spirit is the truth" (1 John 5:6). We are wise to study God's Word and respond to God's Holy Spirit that we may know the Lord.

Called into Fellowship and Freedom

Once we come to know that the Lord is God, we are invited to know that he is good and desires our fellowship. It is not an ogre or author of ill and ugliness that we are drawn to know. The psalmist says: "Taste and see that the Lord is good; blessed is the one who takes refuge in him" (Ps 34:8). Psalms are replete with claims of God's goodness and the beauty of God's creation. Along that line of thinking, the first question of the Westminster Shorter Catechism asks, "What is the chief end of man [sic]?" Answer, "Man's [sic] chief end is to glorify God[7] and to enjoy him forever."[8] Those words speak of a warm, joyful relationship stemming from identifying and praising the ways and the works of God.

Jesus Christ called us into a warm, family-bonded relationship with God when he taught us the Lord's Prayer. Right from its outset we are invited to speak of God as "Our Father which art in heaven." The concept of a father is a far cry from a Supreme Being or Almighty God. Jesus invites us to understand our place as beloved children of God. We are not relegated to an outer circle of acquaintances due to our sin. We may approach God as beloved family. The Heidelberg Catechism asks, "Why did Christ command us to call God 'our Father'?" Answer, "To awaken in us at the very beginning of our prayer what should be basic to our prayer—a childlike reverence and trust that through Christ God has become our Father, and that just as our parents do not refuse

---

7. Ps 86, Isa 60:21, Rom 11:36, 1 Cor 10:31, and Rev 4:11.

8. Ps 16:5–11, 144:15, Isa 12:2, Luke 2:10, Phil 4:4, Rev 21:3–4, and "The Westminster Shorter Catechism," 205.

us the things of this life, even less will God our Father refuse to give us what we ask in faith."[9]

The Westminster Shorter Catechism, Q17, says that we can only know God as God chooses to be made known. That might cause us to despair, wondering if God wants us (individually and specifically) to know him, but we need not worry, "For God so loved the world that he sent his one and only Son, that whoever believes in him shall not perish but have eternal life" (John 3:16). That passage should convince us not to fear that God calls some to condemnation and others to salvation even before we are born.[10] Calvin's logic stemmed from his keen appreciation of God's sovereignty. Indeed, God is sovereign in all matters. Anabaptist theologians understand, however, that Genesis 2–3 demonstrates the allowed struggle between humanity's God-given freewill and God's keen desire for relationship with humanity. The same account also demonstrates the cost of ill-chosen freedom. God would be known by all means. Through God's wooing of humanity by general and specific revelation, we are alerted to God's presence and called to respond. We are not slaves to that call but are invited into fellowship—that we may choose to love the LORD God of the universe.

Called to Love God Only

God's invitation to fellowship is exclusive as seen in the first Commands (Exod 20:1–6; Deut 5:6–10). To our peril we design a god of our preference or accept parts of the LORD and incorporate aspects of other gods and idols. We are called to love the LORD our God only and to practice our faith as God prescribes.

Excellent teaching points on God's exclusive call upon our lives are found in question 94 and 95 of the Heidelberg Catechism.[11]

Q 94. What does the Lord Require in the first Commandment?

---

9. Christian Reformed Church, "The Heidelberg Catechism," 120 Q.
10. Calvin, *Institutes of the Christian Religion*, 3.21.5.
11. Christian Reformed Church, "The Heidelberg Catechism," 94, 95 Q.

A. That I, not wanting to endanger my very salvation, avoid and shun all idolatry, magic, superstitious rites, and prayer to saints or to other creatures. That I sincerely acknowledge the only true God, trust him alone, look to him for every good thing humbly and patiently, love him, fear him, and honor him with all my heart. In short, that I give up anything rather than go against his will in any way.

Q 95. What is idolatry?

A. Idolatry is having or inventing something in which one trusts in place of or alongside of the only true God, who has revealed himself in his Word."

By these words we can understand that syncretism of faith is a result of our sin. It is contrary to God's exclusive call upon our lives. It endangers our eternal standing with God. As the apostle Paul said, "For of this you can be sure: No immoral, impure or greedy person—such a person is an idolater—has any inheritance in the kingdom of Christ and of God" (Eph 5:5).

Called to Teach God's Commands

There is a strong and ongoing mandate from God for humanity to learn and keep his commands. God commanded Joshua to lead the people by using the Law, which Moses passed down, saying, "Keep this Book of the Law always on your lips; meditate on it day and night, so that you may be careful to do everything written in it. Then you will be prosperous and successful" (Josh 1:8). In order to keep God's Law, therefore, one must learn it. The trivial pursuits of this world were therefore to be subdued by the premier values and teachings of God.

Likewise, there is a strong and ongoing mandate from God to pass along and teach God's commands to the generations that follow. Prior to the destruction of Sodom and Gomorrah, Abraham entertained three visitors. At one point the visitors spoke as for God, saying, "For I have chosen him, so that he will direct his children and his household after him to keep the way of the Lord

EPILOGUE—WHY WE TEACH TENETS OF FAITH

by doing what is right and just, so that the LORD will bring about for Abraham what he has promised him" (Gen 18:19). In the midst of being freed from Egyptian slavery Moses said to the people:

> "Obey these instructions as a lasting ordinance for you and your descendants. When you enter the land that the LORD will give you as he promised, observe this ceremony. And when your children ask you, 'What does this ceremony mean to you?' then tell them, 'It is the Passover sacrifice to the LORD, who passed over the houses of the Israelites in Egypt and spared our homes when he struck down the Egyptians.' Then the people bowed down and worshiped." (Exod 12:24–27)

The question arises, however, what is the best way to fulfill the mandate to teach succeeding generations?

Though Sunday schools had their origins in the 1780s among unchurched urban children in England[12] and cheders had their origins in Europe for Jewish children to be taught Hebrew and Torah about the same time,[13] there was teaching of young Jewish children much earlier. Jesus must have been taught scripture as a youth in the home or synagogue.[14] Scripture leads us to believe that Jesus was a bright and avid student. He had learned much scripture by the time he was twelve years old. "Everyone who heard him was amazed at his understanding and his answers" (v. 47 of Luke 2:41–52). By the time he was preaching and teaching in his ministry, he was commonly called rabbi/teacher; those words are found 123 times in the gospels.

---

12. Larsen, "When Did Sunday Schools Start?" *Christianity Today: Christian History*, accessed December 2, 2017, http://www.christianitytoday.com/history/2008/august/when-did-sunday-schools-start.html.

13. "Cheder," *Wikipedia*, accessed December 2, 2017, https://en.wikipedia.org/wiki/Cheder.

14. Contrary to common prejudice against residents of Galilee, one source believes the area was highly religious during Jesus' time with an active program of religious training. "Rabbi and Talmidim," *That the World May Know: Focus On the Family*, accessed December 2, 2017, https://www.thattheworldmayknow.com/rabbi-and-talmidim.

TEACHING TENETS OF FAITH IN WORSHIP

Teaching God's word is the sacred call for all believers so that others may know. We are each to meditate upon God's word and discuss God's way with people throughout each day. Parents are to instruct their children. We are to share our faith as God said through Moses:

> "Hear, O Israel: The LORD our God, the LORD is one. Love the LORD your God with all your heart and with all your soul and with all your strength. These commandments that I give you today are to be on your hearts. Impress them on your children. Talk about them when you sit at home and when you walk along the road, when you lie down and when you get up. Tie them as symbols on your hands and bind them on your foreheads. Write them on the doorframes of your houses and on your gates." (Deut 6:4–9)

As we do these things, the prophet says we do something lovely. "How beautiful on the mountains are the feet of those who bring good news, who proclaim peace, who bring good tidings, who proclaim salvation, who say to Zion, "Your God reigns!" (Isa 52:7). Paul echoes those words: "And how can anyone preach unless they are sent? As it is written: 'How beautiful are the feet of those who bring good news'" (Rom 10:15).

God commanded his leaders and all believers to teach the people so that they would know God. When Moses spent too much time in administrative activity, Jethro said:

> "What you are doing is not good. You and these people who come to you will only wear yourselves out. The work is too heavy for you; you cannot handle it alone. Listen now to me and I will give you some advice, and may God be with you. You must be the people's representative before God and bring their disputes to him. Teach them his decrees and instructions, and show them the way they are to live and how they are to behave. But select capable men from all the people [to be judges and handle the people's administrative needs]." (Exod 18:17–21)

EPILOGUE—WHY WE TEACH TENETS OF FAITH

Teaching was sacred duty. "Only be careful, and watch yourselves closely so that you do not forget the things your eyes have seen or let them fade from your heart as long as you live. Teach them to your children and to their children after them" (Deut 4:9).

Though all believers are to share their faith and teach their children, some are called specially to that ministry. In the Old Testament, priests and religious leaders were tasked with teaching. "For a long time Israel was without the true God, without a priest to teach and without the law" (2 Chr 15:3). In Nehemiah 8, we see the great teacher, Ezra, in the act of teaching God's Law in Jerusalem to the whole assembled post-exile gathering of Israelites.

The New Testament affirms the special call of teachers. Jesus' last word to his apostles before his ascension was the command to teach.

> "Therefore go and make disciples of all nations, baptizing them in the name of the Father and of the Son and of the Holy Spirit, and teaching them to obey everything I have commanded you. And surely I am with you always, to the very end of the age." (Matt 28:19–20)

There can also be commissioning for teaching specific groups of people. Paul said, "And for this purpose I was appointed a herald . . . and faithful teacher of the Gentiles." (1 Tim 2:7)

A great majority of scriptural references are about "teachers of the law." We see that scope broadened to teach Christ's ways (as Matt 28 above) and in 1 Corinthians 12:28 and Ephesians 4:11, among others. However, since Christ did not come to abolish the law (Matt 5:17), another way of thinking is that Christ's way and commands are now part of the Law. Anabaptists understand that Jesus' commands and life example is the lens through which we are to interpret all scripture.[15]

We are instructed by Jesus' words to teachers of the Law that we must be pliable to follow the Holy Spirit; we may not cling to

---

15. Article 4 says, " . . . Led by the Holy Spirit in the church, we interpret Scripture in harmony with Jesus Christ," in *Confession of Faith in a Mennonite Perspective: A Summary Statement* (Scottdale, PA: Herald Press, 1995), Article #4.

old understandings merely because they follow our tradition. Indeed, our teaching must be summarized in sound doctrine. "You, however, must teach what is appropriate to sound doctrine" (Titus 2:1). James reminds us of the responsibility inherent in teaching. "Not many of you should become teachers, my fellow believers, because you know that we who teach will be judged more strictly" (Jas 3:1).

Pedagogy: Biblical Teaching Methods Provided Us

This text proffers a method of introducing, correcting, and reinforcing elements of Christian faith within the context of worship. The goal is to create a clearer and more orthodox understanding of Christ's Way. Teaching in worship has a strong theological and biblical basis. What follows are examples of teaching in both Old and New Testaments.

Prime in our understanding of what pleases God comes from the accounts of Creation and Fall (Gen 1–3). Here we learn that God created and called all things "good." Creation pleased God very much. We learn it is wiser to honor what God has made and what God commands than to go our own way. We stray from God's commands to our peril. Such stories are found in every book of the Old Testament,[16] each for the purpose of conveying truths about God and humankind.

The codified law for God's Chosen People is found in Leviticus, Numbers, and Deuteronomy. The people were encouraged to learn and obey the law so as to please God and live long. It was God's call to Moses' and the leaders that followed him, to teach God's laws. Deuteronomy 5:31 says, "But you, stand here by me, and I will tell you all the commandments, the statutes and the ordinances, that you shall teach them, so that they may do them in the land that I am giving them to possess." We are to understand that God's leaders are called to make sure the people know, remember, and obey God's Law. God's leaders do not merely lead, they teach.

---

16. Teaching via story form is found even in the law, Leviticus, Numbers, and Deuteronomy. The Law and wisdom books such as Psalms, Proverbs, and Ecclesiastes are peppered with stories and visual snippets to capture the imagination and heart.

EPILOGUE—WHY WE TEACH TENETS OF FAITH

Admonishment and exhortation are prime roles of the prophets. It is important to remember, however, that those devices were also used in the story form and codified portions of the Law. As an example, Cain was confronted, admonished, and punished for his murder of Abel (Gen 4) and Aaron's sons, Nadab and Abihu, died when offering unholy fire amid priestly duties, thus becoming ex-humus admonishment to Aaron's remaining sons to perform their priestly duties faithfully (Num 3). As Moses prepared the people to enter the Promised Land, he exhorted them to put their best foot forward to please God so they would live long and prosperously in that land. Deuteronomy 26:16 says, "This very day the LORD your God is commanding you to observe these statutes and ordinances; so observe them diligently with all your heart and with all your soul."

As for the prophets, their tone was most often one of corrective admonishment for failing to live up to God's covenant. The prophets stood as teachers who spoke of impending punishment if the people would not turn from their errant ways. Jeremiah and Hosea are perhaps harshest, but each of the prophets in turn admonished the people powerfully.

There are gentler moments among the prophets where God exhorts rather than admonishes the people to repent and follow him to find peace with God. Jonah stands as an example of story form exhortation. Rather than pointing God's judgmental finger at Judah and Israel, God focused on the notoriously sinful Nineveh, part of Assyria. Upon Jonah's prophetic work, Nineveh's king repented and all Nineveh with him. The lesson for all listeners and readers of Jonah's story is that God may relent at our repentance. Through the teaching of Jonah, it should be no surprise that God extends his message of mercy and grace to all peoples.

God's people are not free to fashion a syncretistic faith. That is a taint that God does not accept. God's people are called to hold on to one true faith as described in scripture. God's condemnation of idolatry through the oscillating stories of the Book of Judges, the histories of Judah's and Israel's unfaithful kingdoms, and the

TEACHING TENETS OF FAITH IN WORSHIP

words of the prophets show us that our faith is to be in the LORD God alone. We are taught:

> "Hear, O Israel: The LORD our God, the LORD is one . . . You shall have no other gods before me. You shall not make for yourself an image in the form of anything in heaven above or on the earth beneath or in the waters below." (Deut 6:4 and 5:7-8)

Jesus is considered by many to have been a master of teaching theological truth. He employed outright commands (Matt 7). He used stories to illuminate truth (Matthew 4:19). He created morals from episodes in their lives (Luke 21). He used parables (Matt 20:1-16). The gospels contain very little of his outright preaching, making it all the more powerful because of its rarity, including the Sermon on the Mount (Matt 5-7) and "sermon on the plain" (Luke 6).

The gospels illustrate that Jesus' favored teaching approach was through story, simile, and parable to invoke his listeners' imagination and continued meditative thinking. Epic in their power to fascinate and teach us truths down through the ages are Jesus' stories of the farmer who sewed seeds and the results (Mark 4), the Prodigal Son (Luke 15), the Judge who gave righteous judgment because of the woman's persistence (Luke 18:1-8), and the separation of sheep from goats due to their prior actions (Matt 25:31-46).

We see in the Book of Acts and in the epistles, that Stephen, Peter, and Paul were preachers and teachers who used story form as they spoke of their history with Jesus, but they never used parable or illustration. Their preaching styles seem to make no time for more sophisticated teaching approaches (Acts 2:14-36, 3:12-26, 4:8-20, 7, 17:22-31, 21:40—22:1, 21, 24:10-21, and 26:1-23). Philip's teaching, on the other hand, is more nuanced. Acts 8:5 says he proclaimed. Acts 8:26-35 says that he listened to the Ethiopian eunuch reading scripture; he asked a simple question: "Do you understand what you are reading?" (v. 30), which opened the door to Philip providing scriptural context and explaining its meaning.

EPILOGUE—WHY WE TEACH TENETS OF FAITH

Jesus and the epistle writers acted as interpreters of the Law and therefore taught their listeners about God's Law. They provided correctives to teach us of the initial intent of particular commands and also of additional lessons one can gain from them. Jesus said:

> "'You shall love the Lord your God with all your heart, and with all your soul, and with all your mind.' This is the greatest and first commandment. And a second is like it: 'You shall love your neighbor as yourself.' On these two commandments hang all the law and the prophets."
> (Matt 22:37–40)

By Jesus' interpretation we understand many lessons: that God and God's Law are premier, that all scripture ties together, that we must hold tight to God and refrain from other gods, and that we should not get so deep into the minutia of the Law that we forget that its highest calling is to love both God and neighbor without exclusion.

Paul helps us understand the usefulness of the Law when he claims that its primary role is to convince us of our deep need for salvation and grace from God through Jesus Christ (Rom, especially 3:20, 4:13, 5:20, 8:2). Each epistle writer helps us understand our need for salvation through Jesus Christ by appealing through God's Hebraic Law, as above, or by God's general revelation. In keeping with Isaiah's example (40:21), Paul spoke through what he saw in creation (1 Cor 15:40–49).

Jesus and the epistle writers admonished and exhorted their listeners to follow truly the ways of God. Jesus most often spoke to his disciples in the intimate manner of a beloved teacher with students (Matt 13:36–43). He also allowed outsiders to listen (Matt 5–7). He reserved his harshest admonitions for those who were unwilling to listen because they thought they were already righteous (Matt 23).

Jesus and his disciples set the example for all the subsequent church leaders, preachers, and teachers that follow. We are to instruct, teach, preach, and correct for the benefit of righteousness, always pointing to Christ, and challenging the false teachings of the age.

Bibliography

Allen, Ronald J. *Wholly Scripture: Preaching Biblical Themes*. St. Louis, Mo: Chalice, 2004.

Babcock, Maltbie D. "This Is My Father's World" (public domain, 1901).

Barna. *Gen Z: The Culture, Beliefs and Motivations Shaping the Next Generation*. [location not listed]: Barna Group and Impact 360 Institute, 2018.

Benson, Bruce. *Liturgy As A Way of Life: Embodying the Arts in Christian Worship*. Grand Rapids, MI: Baker Academic, 2013.

Boers, Arthur Paul, Barbara Nelson Gingerich, Eleanor Kreider, John Rempel, and Mary H. Schertz. *Take Our Moments and Our Days: An Anabaptist Prayer Book, Ordinary Time*. Scottdale, PA: Herald, 2007.

Boers, Arthur Paul, Barbara Nelson Gingerich, Eleanor Kreider, John Rempel, and Mary H. Schertz. *Take Our Moments and Our Days: An Anabaptist Prayer Book, Volume 2: Advent through Pentecost*. Scottdale, PA: Herald, 2010.

Bradley, C. Randall. *From Memory to Imagination: Reforming the Church's Music*. Grand Rapids, MI: Eerdmans, 2012.

Bratt, James D., ed. *Viewpoints: Exploring the Reformed Vision*. Grand Rapids, MI: CRC, 1992.

Brown, Anthony, and Pat Barrett. "Good, Good Father." Capitol CMG Publishing, 2014.

Brenneman, Diane Zaerr. *Words for Worship 2*. Scottdale, PA: Herald, 2009.

Buegler, Todd. "Why Is No One Talking About This?" *The Network: The ELCA Youth Ministry Network*, December 2, 2013, accessed January 26, 2016, https://elcaymnet.wordpress.com/2013/12/02/why-is-no-one-talking-about-this/.

Calvin, John. *Institutes of the Christian Religion: Volume II*. Translated by Henry Beveridge. Grand Rapids, MI: Wm. B. Eerdmans, 1970.

Carden, Paul, ed. *Christianity, Cults, & Religions, 7th Edition*. Torrance, CA: Rose, 1996.

Chan, Francis. *Crazy Love: Overwhelmed By A Relentless God*. Colorado Springs: David C. Cook, 2013.

BIBLIOGRAPHY

Chan, Simon. *Liturgical Theology: The Church as Worshiping Community.* Downers Grove, IL: IVP, 2006.

Chesterton, G.K. *Orthodoxy.* New York: Image, 1959.

Christian Reformed Church in North America. "The Heidelberg Catechism." *Psalter Hymnal: Doctrinal Standards and Liturgy of the Christian Reformed Church,* 7–68. Grand Rapids, MI: Board of Publications of the Christian Reformed Church, 1976.

Church of England. *The Book of Common Prayer and Administration of the Sacraments and Other Rites and Ceremonies of the Church: Together with the Psalter or Psalms of David.* New York: Oxford University Press, 2007.

Currie, David A. *The Big Idea of Biblical Worship: The Development & Leadership of Expository Services.* Peabody, MA: Hendrickson, 2017.

Devillers, Sylvia. *Lectionary-Based Catechesis for Children: A Catechist's Guide.* New York: Paulist, 1994.

Dirkx, John M. "Transformative Learning Theory in the Practice of Adult Education: An Overview." *PAACE Journal of Lifelong Learning* 7 (1998) 1–14, https://www.iup.edu/WorkArea/DownloadAsset.aspx?id=18335.

Dooley, Sr. Catherine. "Remembering the Future: Memory and Imagination." *Proceedings of the 13th Annual National Association of Parish Catechetical Directors (NPCD) Convocation* (Philadelphia, March 29 – April 1, 2005) 1–10. Washington, DC: National Catholic Educational Association, 2006.

Dooley, Kate. "The Lectionary as a Sourcebook of Catechesis in the Catechumenate." In *Before and After Baptism: The Work of Teachers and Catechists,* edited by James A. Wilde, 39–51. Chicago: Liturgy Training, 1988.

Focus On the Family. "Rabbi and Talmidim." *That the World May Know with Ray Vander Laan.* Accessed December 2, 2017. https://www.thattheworldmayknow.com/rabbi-and-talmidim.

General Conference Mennonite Church and Mennonite Church. *Confession of Faith in a Mennonite Perspective.* Scottdale, PA: Herald, 1995.

Getty, Keith, and Kristyn Getty. *Sing! How Worship Transforms Your Life, Family, and Church.* Nashville, TN: B&H Books, Getty Music Songs, LLC, 2017, 2, 10.

Graffagnino, Jason J. "The Shaping of the Two Earliest Anabaptist Catechisms." PhD diss., Southwestern Baptist Theological Seminary, 2008.

Grieser, Jeanne and Carol Duerksen. *Adventures With the Anabaptists: A Study for Youth.* Newton, KS: Faith and Life Resources, 2002.

Hall, Jennifer Lea. "Syncretism." Master's thesis, Virginia Commonwealth University, 2008.

Herald Press. *Confession of Faith in a Mennonite Perspective: A Summary Statement.* Scottdale, PA: Herald, 1995.

Hershberger, Michele. *God's Story, Our Story: Exploring Christian Faith & Life.* Scottdale, PA: Faith and Life Resources, 2013.

Heschel, Abraham Joshua. *The Sabbath.* New York: Farrar, Straus and Giroux, 1979.

BIBLIOGRAPHY

Horton, Michael. *A Better Way: Rediscovering the Drama of God-Centered Worship*. Grand Rapids, MI: Baker, 2002.

Immink, F. Gerrit. *The Touch of the Sacred: The Practice, Theology, and Tradition of Christian Worship*. Grand Rapids, MI: William B. Eerdmans, 2014.

Jager, Ronald. *The Development of Bertrand Russell's Philosophy*. New York: Humanities, 1972. https://books.google.de/books?id=QYoqD-27T50C&pg=PA257&lpg=PA257&dq=to+name+something&source=bl&ots=HZeoh5yCOz&sig=RXUdyMLSDiYdeo4pU18P5ucoJZg&hl=en&sa=X&red ir_esc=y#v=onepage&q&f=true.

Keller, Timothy, and Sam Shammas. *New City Catechism*. New York: Redeemer Presbyterian Church, 2012.

Kidd, Reggie. *With One Voice: Discovering Christ's Song in Our Worship*. Grand Rapids, MI: Baker, 2005.

Kohler, Jamie Nichole. "Preaching the Gospel to All: Using Multiple Intelligence Theory to Catechize." Master's thesis, Saint Mary's University of Minnesota, 2004.

Komonchak, Joseph A. "The Authority of the Catechism." In *Introducing the Catechism of the Catholic Church: Traditional Themes and Contemporary Issues*, edited by Berard L. Marthaler, 22. New York: Paulist, 1994.

Kreider, Alan. *The Patient Ferment of the Early Church: The Improbable Rise of Christianity in the Roman Empire*. Grand Rapids, MI: Baker Academic, 2016.

Kuyvenhoven, Andrew. *Comfort & Joy: A Study of the Heidelberg Catechism*. Grand Rapids, MI: CRC, 1988.

Labberton, Mark. *The Dangerous Act of Worship: Living God's Call to Justice*. Downers Grove, IL: IVP, 2007.

Larsen, Timothy. "When Did Sunday Schools Start?" *Christianity Today: Christian History* (August 2008). http://www.christianitytoday.com/history/2008/august/when-did-sunday-schools-start.html.

Loewen, Howard John. *One Lord, One Church, One Hope, and One God: Mennonite Confessions of Faith, Text-Reader Series No. 2*. [location not cited]: Institute of Mennonite Studies, 1985.

Mark, Arlene M. *Words for Worship*. Scottdale, PA: Herald, 1996.

McKim, Donald K. *Presbyterian Questions, Presbyterian Answers: Exploring Christian Faith*. Louisville, KY: Geneva, 2003.

Mennonite Church USA. *Claim(ing) Faith: Youth Discover the Confession of Faith*. Harrisonburg, VA: MennoMedia, 2013.

Neufeld, Alfred. *What We Believe Together: Exploring the "Shared Convictions" of Anabaptist-Related Churches*. New York: Good, 2015.

Packer, J. I., and Gary A. Parrett. *Grounded in the Gospel: Building Believers the Old-Fashioned Way*. Grand Rapids, MI: Baker, 2010.

Parry, Robin. *Worshiping Trinity: Coming Back to the Heart of Worship*. Eugene, OR: Cascade, 2012.

Plantinga, Jr., Cornelius. *Beyond Doubt: Faith-building Devotions on Questions Christians Ask*. Grand Rapids, MI: William B. Eerdmans, 2002.

BIBLIOGRAPHY

Powell, Karan H., and Joseph P. Sinwell. *Breaking Open the Word of God: Resources for Using the Lectionary for Catechesis in the RCIA Cycle C*. New York: Paulist, 1988.

Presbyterian Church USA. *Catechism for Young Children: An Introduction to the Shorter Catechism*. Lawrenceville, GA: Christian Education and Publications, [date unlisted].

———. "The Westminster Shorter Catechism." *Book of Confessions: The Constitution of the Presbyterian Church (USA), Part 1*, 203–221. Louisville, KY: The Office of the General Assembly, 2014.

Rienstra, Debra and Ron Rienstra. *Worship Words: Discipling Language for Faithful Ministry*. Grand Rapids, MI: Baker Academic, 2009.

Rosier, Veronica C. *Liturgical Catechesis of Sunday Celebrations in the Absence of a Priest*. Sterling, VA: Peeters, 2000.

Ross, Melanie. *Evangelical Versus Liturgical: Defying a Dichotomy*. Grand Rapids, MI: Eerdmans, 2014.

Schaller, Lyle E., ed. *Creative Leadership Series: Teaching the Bible to Adults and Youth*. By Dick Murray. Nashville, TN: Abingdon, 1987.

Schmit, Clayton. *Sent and Gathered: A Worship Manual for the Missional Church*. Grand Rapids, MI: Baker Academic, 2009.

Schütz, Johann J. "Sei Lob und Ehr dem hochsten Gut," translated by France E. Cox. In Hymnal: A Worship Book, 59. Elgin, IL: Brethren Press, 1982.

Shenk, Calvin E. *Who Do You Say That I Am? Christians Encounter Other Religions*. Scottdale, PA: Herald, 1997.

Sloyan, Gerard S. "Forming Catechumens through the Lectionary." In *Before and After Baptism: The Work of Teachers and Catechists*, edited by James A. Wilde, 27–37. Chicago: Liturgy Training, 1988.

Sloyan, Gerard S. "The Homily and Catechesis: The Catechism and/or the Lectionary?" In *Introducing the Catechism of the Catholic Church: Traditional Themes and Contemporary Issues*, edited by Bernard L. Marthaler, 133–141. Mahwah, NJ: Paulist, 1994.

Smith, Christian. "On 'Moralistic Therapeutic Deism' as U.S. Teenagers' Actual, Tacit, De Facto Religious Faith." *The Princeton Lectures on Youth, Church, and Culture* (2005). Accessed January 11, 2016. http://www.ptsem.edu/lectures/?action=results&by=creator&qtext=creator%3a%22Smith,+Christian%22+sort%3atitle.

Smith, Christian, and Melinda Lindquist Denton. *Soul Searching: The Religious and Spiritual Lives of American Teenagers*. New York: Oxford University Press, 2005.

Smith, James K. A. *Imagining the Kingdom: How Worship Works*. Grand Rapids, MI: Baker Academic, 2013.

Stump, Joseph. *An Explanation of Luther's Small Catechism*. Philadelphia: Fortress, 1960.

Stutzman, Ervin R. *From Nonresistance to Justice: The Transformation of Mennonite Church Peace Rhetoric 1908-2008*. Scottdale, PA: Herald, 2011.

BIBLIOGRAPHY

Torrance, James. *Worship, Community, and the Triune God of Grace.* Downers Grove, IL: IVP, 1996.

Torrey, R. A. *The Holy Spirit: Who He Is And What He Does And How to Know Him In All the Fullness of His Gracious and Glorious Ministry.* Greenville, SC: Ambassador International, 2006.

Tozer, A. W. *The Attributes of God, Volume I with Study Guide.* Camp Hill, PA: Wing Spread, 2003.

Tripp, Paul. *A Quest for Something More: Living for Something Bigger than You* Greensboro, NC: New Growth, 2007, 145.

Waisanen, Cori McMillin. "Crossing the Great Divide: Syncretism Or Contextualization in Christian Worship." DMiss diss., Asbury Theological Seminary, 2010.

Watson, Hillary. "Sunday School is Dying." *Mennonite World Review* no. 19 (Sept 10, 2018): 5.

Weaver, Dorothy Jean. *The Irony of Power: The Politics of God Within Matthew's Narrative.* Eugene, OR: Pickwick, 2017.

Wikipedia. "Cheder." Accessed December 2, 2017. https://en.wikipedia.org/wiki/Cheder.

Wilde, James A., ed. *Before And After Baptism: The Work of Teachers and Catechists.* Chicago: Liturgy Training, 1988.

Witvliet, John. *Worship Seeking Understanding: Windows into Christian Practice.* Grand Rapids, MI: Baker Academic, 2003.

Wolterstorff, Nicholas. *Hearing the Call: Liturgy, Justice, Church, and World.* Edited by Gornik and Thompson. Grand Rapids, MI: William B. Eerdmans, 2011.

Wright, N. T. *For All God's Worth: True Worship and the Calling of the Church.* Grand Rapids, MI: Eerdmans, 1997.

Yamasaki, April. *Making Disciples: Preparing People for Baptism, Christian Living, and Church Membership.* Newton, KS: Faith and Life Resources, 2003.

About the Author

James Åkerson is a pastor of a rural congregation and district minister for the Virginia Mennonite Conference (MCUSA). In 2015, James authored *Celebrating 80 Years of Ministry: The Missional Story of Beldor Church*. He earned his Doctor of Ministry from Gordon-Conwell Theological Seminary in Massachusetts, where the basis of this worship lectionary was conceived. Earlier, he earned his Master of Divinity from Eastern Mennonite Seminary in Virginia. He is a "convinced" Anabaptist. Born in Oregon, he was raised in the Lutheran tradition where he gained an appreciation for high-church practices of worship. He and his wife, Emily, have two grown sons, Lars and Nels. James and his family enjoy sailing on inland lakes and the Chesapeake Bay.

James devoted 35 years to a career as forester and ecologist, tending the forestlands of Liberia, West Africa, Oregon and America's West, and Virginia's Blue Ridge Mountains. In those years he has worked with the U.S. Peace Corps, U.S. Bureau of Indian Affairs, and U.S. National Park Service. He has authored several forest management texts. James holds a high view that all Christian believers are called to care for Creation. He serves as a volunteer along the Appalachian National Scenic Trial where he leads groups in controlling invasive vegetation.

www.ingramcontent.com/pod-product-compliance
Lightning Source LLC
Chambersburg PA
CBHW070921160426
43193CB00011B/1553